MIND THE GAP!

An Insider's Irreverent Look
at Private School Finances
and Management–
with a Lesson for Government
and Industry, Too!

Dr. Richard J. Soghoian

D0089259

More Acclaim for Richard Soghoian's
Mind the Gap!

"Riveting. Once I started, I could not put it down....It will definitely put everyone else to shame, but hopefully, will show them how to cut the waste and find a way out of the financial mess we are in, especially the school systems, private and public included. Your book puts everything out so simply. It was readable, understandable, and I know it will be a tremendous success."

> —Rona Kirsh Davis, Board of Trustees Member and Parent, Columbia Grammar and Preparatory School, NY

"It is quite a talent to infuse optimism and positive energy into a subject matter where you are essentially exposing something quite disturbing for a parent. I learned so much about our own school as well as the unbelievable practices of the general private school administrative community. *Mind the Gap!* was incredibly eye-opening... I know every parent in our community will feel this way upon reading it. And every one of them should read it voraciously."

> —Suzanne Lindbergh, Parent, Columbia Grammar and Preparatory School, NY

"Excellent! Eye-opening!...I applaud you for bucking the system and doing it your way — the correct way. It probably will have short-term backlash, but I would still go public with your findings and philosophies — as that is the only way the entire system will change."

> —Jonathan Rosen, Former Parent, Columbia Grammar and Preparatory School, NY

"Perhaps the greatest pleasure I got in reading your piece was to see what a wonderful school you have built — both the description of the physical plant as well as the solid operating principles which you have inculcated in its management. Knowing I had a tiny contribution to make way back at the beginning remains a source of great personal satisfaction to me."

> —David P. Steinman, Former Board of Trustees President, Columbia Grammar and Preparatory School, NY

"Very stimulating, and you have asked provocative questions in order to make your points....I think that parents at these other schools should rightfully be disturbed to know that their generous contributions actually go towards perpetuating the habits of bloat and inefficiency."

> —Clifford Press, Former Parent, Columbia Grammar and Preparatory School, NY

Columbia Grammar and Preparatory School
5 West 93rd Street
New York, NY 10025
212-749-6200, www.cgps.org

The author has donated this book with
love and appreciation to
Columbia Grammar and Preparatory School.

All proceeds go to the *Mind the Gap!* Fund.

A NOTE TO READERS

Through Dr. Richard Soghoian's three decades of innovative leadership, Columbia Grammar and Preparatory School has experienced unprecedented growth and renewal, which Dr. Soghoian expertly chronicles in this well-received and informative book (now in paperback). The Columbia Grammar and Preparatory School Board of Trustees is committed to sharing Dr. Soghoian's successful financial and management philosophy with as many schools, colleges and organizations as possible to enable these institutions to continue to prosper in the face of increasing financial pressures and uncertainties. To this end, the Board of Trustees has established the *Mind the Gap!* Fund, which will support travel, lodging, and related expenses to enable Dr. Soghoian to speak and consult as his schedule allows. For additional information, contact Alida Clemans, Editor, at aclemans@cgps.org.

Sincerely,

Andrew Zaro
President, Board of Trustees
Columbia Grammar and Preparatory School
New York City

CONTENTS

ACKNOWLEDGEMENTS

In spite of the many requests I have had over recent years to tell this story, the main reason I have been reluctant to do so has to do mainly with what George Herbert Walker Bush referred to in his own autobiography as "The Big I Am." It is difficult if not impossible to avoid the over-emphasis on the "I" in this sort of circumstance where leading a school for a period of three decades (and counting), especially from a state of insolvency to a position of success, has centered on my own efforts in virtually every area of school life. Try as I might, therefore, I have been unable to avoid the self-serving and at times unbecoming over-use of the "I" in this narrative.

But over and over again, the school's success, while dependent in an obvious way on my own efforts, could not and would not have occurred without the timely and generous help of literally dozens and dozens of individuals along the way. So one of the great pleasures of telling this story is the opportunity to thank—beginning with my loving, intelligent, wise, and infinitely supportive wife—the countless individuals, mostly parents, who stepped forward just when most needed—what the Ancient Greeks called *kairos*, the perfect moment.

Too many individuals to name in full deserve a place of honor in this 30-year history of growth and renewal, but the following played roles so important that if any one of them had not come forward to help at that perfect moment, the history, at least the history worth telling, would have stopped as well. Each one of these individuals represents what we refer to in formal logic as a "necessary" as opposed to a "sufficient" cause of an event, in this case, the very survival of Columbia Grammar and Prep School.

• Doris Rosenblum, Community Organizer Supreme of the Upper West Side and Manager of Community Board #7. Doris quite literally never took "no" for an answer—and the "yeses" all added up to opening many critical doors to our future.

• Nan Miller, Assistant Vice President at Chemical Bank, who took an inexplicable gamble on this headmaster and this little bankrupt school on the Upper West Side to provide a generous construction loan for our first new building—a leap of faith that to this day tests my innate skepticism about banks and similar financial institutions, but also continually renews my faith in mankind.

• Hirschel Abelson, treasurer of the board of trustees starting my second year, for the crucial first decade of my tenure. Hirschel was critical to putting our financial house in order when it was in total disorder, and he gave the first of many leadership gifts in those early days when voluntary giving was still an alien idea to the school community.

• David Steinmann, president of the board for most of those crucial first 10 years, laid the groundwork for a strong and active board. Brilliant, articulate, and imposing in stature, David gave us our first taste of the big leagues of New York City private education, and his leadership translated into growing success, all with a sophistication and confidence that has defined our school—and very directly the Board of Trustees—to this day.

• Peter Reynolds, as Chief Financial Officer, reorganized our operating budget from top to bottom and made sure it stayed that way—lean and efficient. Peter had a wonderful combination of old-fashioned pragmatism on the one hand and philosophical wisdom on the other, as comfortable with budgets and administrative detail as he was with Descartes and Krishnamurti.

• Carl Morse, owner and president of Morse Diesel, now known as AMEC Construction Management, Inc., one of the preeminent management construction companies in the history of America. Carl took on our first and most critical building project while in his 80s, retired but still tough and cantankerous as ever, bullied the unions into doing work on time and on budget, and essentially put himself and his reputation on the line to see that our building was built in one year, for the start of school in the fall of 1985.

ACKNOWLEDGEMENTS

• Alice Rosenwald, the personification of *kairos*, who indeed appeared at the perfect moment when I had a wonderful idea, but not the financial means to make it a reality. Today, if it were not for Alice, our school would not have the finest program within a program to educate bright, learning disabled students, and hundreds of colleges and universities would have lost the opportunity to have these remarkable students grace their campuses.

• Peter and Mary Kalikow, two of the most philanthropic people ever produced by a city filled with philanthropic individuals, deserve our eternal thanks for two extraordinary new buildings for our school—72,000 square feet of the finest space—and the Learning Resource Center, which has given literally hundreds of capable children with learning disabilities an opportunity to get the (very best) education each deserved in a world, the private school world of New York City, quite accustomed to closing its doors to such students. Peter and Mary have left their generous mark on literally every child who has attended our school for the past 20 years, and forever into the future.

• Jerry Heymann, parent, trustee, and President of the Board, whose extraordinary generosity and support, always in the background and understated, provided the long-term and rock-solid personal support (cumulatively around $2 million) to make certain that every one of our projects, large or small, became a success and was completed on time—or well in advance, and whose ironical sense of humor can be found between the lines, so to speak, throughout this book.

• Neil Crespi, parent, trustee, treasurer, and then President of the Board for a 20-year period, leading the way for ever-greater capital giving on the part of trustees and parents alike, culminating in a successful $20 million campaign over the past three years alone, a period of time when many of the other schools experienced a significant decline in giving and an almost across-the-board freeze on capital projects and spending. Our school, on the other hand, redoubled its efforts to achieve complete success—the purchase and renovation of three more brownstones and a $22.5 million renewal of the lower school—thanks first and foremost to Neil Crespi's generosity and leadership.

- Dr. Arturo Constantiner, who as trustee, Vice President, and finally President of the Board, supported our every effort to improve the school in ways large and small and, as the father of three, led the way in providing greater support for teachers and staff—substantially better salaries and benefits for nine years in a row, by far the highest in the city during his tenure. To this day, the school, and certainly this headmaster, enjoys his uniquely warm perspective and unwavering commitment to our school.

- Dr. Larry Howard, parent and President of the Board, who along with Neil Crespi, elevated the meaning of philanthropy to a new level here at our school and created at the same time an esprit de corps among trustees that has made board meetings, especially for this headmaster, something to look forward to with pleasure. Thanks to Dr. Howard, the board today has the membership, structure, and foundation it needs for a strong and secure future—and the inevitable transition to new leadership in the not too distant future.

- Andrew Zaro is the essence of bold and innovative new leadership. As our President of the Board today, Andrew is determined not only to see our school become the finest private school possible, but to ensure that our model becomes a catalyst for change and discussion throughout the private school community.

In short, this story, more than anything, is the story of a community effort, and the "Big I Am" should always be interpreted as a "Big We Did," with the "we" representing the ever-changing and continuing energy, enthusiasm, and voluntary efforts, not only of those named above, but of countless other individuals who helped in ways large and small to make this wonderful story possible over the past 30 years.

It is to this community that this work is dedicated.

This book is about a transformation, by all appearances just short of miraculous, of a small Manhattan private school of approximately 400 students, tucked away on the Upper West Side and literally insolvent in 1981, into one of the most selective and respected private schools in New York City today. In those early years, we routinely admitted, as a matter of survival, virtually anyone who applied (though not everyone accepted us), while today we must cut off applications at 600 for 28-30 spots in kindergarten alone from all five New York City boroughs and beyond. Over a 30-year period, we completed three major new buildings and renovated from top to bottom four empty brownstones (a fifth will be started soon) for a total of 155,000 square feet of new space and actual capital costs of over $75 million (well over $200 million in today's dollars). We raised starting teacher salaries from the bottom tier of private schools in New York City back in 1981 to the very top today, averaging in the past seven years alone nearly 9 percent a year in salary increases, the highest by far of any school in New York City, public or private. We were the very first private school in the city to offer a starting teacher with no experience $60,000 and next year, 2012-2013, we will be the first to start a teacher with no experience at $70,000.

We also greatly improved medical and retirement benefits and doubled our contribution to faculty pensions from 4 to 8 percent and, at the same time, became one of only a small handful of private schools in New York City to pay more than 65 percent of family medical coverage while paying 100 percent of single coverage. We did all of this and much more while accumulating nearly $10 million in endowment—without ever having had an endowment campaign as such—almost as a side-thought.

Today, we have a physical plant valued at well over $200 million *without a single dollar of debt or a single foot of deferred maintenance*. And best of all, our support for an economically and culturally diverse student body grew from a modest 10 percent of our population in 1981 to a representative 23 percent, with a record $5.3 million in financial aid awarded for the year 2011-2012 alone.

Just how we did all this—and much more—is the subject of this book.

The short answer, however, is simply that we learned a very long time ago, out of necessity more than anything else, how to live *on tuition alone*. Tuition alone, you ask? Doesn't everyone operate that way? Well, you might be surprised to learn that in fact *no* other private independent school does so, at least among those in New York City, and to the best of my knowledge, anywhere else for that matter. *All other private independent schools are dependent on annual giving to balance their operating budgets, and many, if not most, are dependent on substantial infusions of interest from endowment funds, as well.*

That indeed is the short answer: We learned early on, out of necessity at first, but voluntarily as the years unfolded, how to live on tuition alone and to use all voluntary gifts—totalling nearly $75 million over these three decades—for capital projects alone. In other words, we never allowed ourselves the luxury of using a dollar of voluntary giving to supplement our operating budget—or to "close the gap," to use the euphemism of private school fundraising. Our mantra or operating philosophy is neatly summarized in the following proposition: *Tuition is for the present, voluntary giving for the future*.

Now, you are understandably wondering how such a simple proposition can possibly account for three decades of extraordinary growth and renewal for our school? The fact is, however, that this simple, unambiguous, and on the face of it, innocuous principle lies not only at the heart of our success as a school over the years, but accounts for much of the financial pressures that are continuously challenging other private schools—and indeed, even more so colleges and universities, especially during these turbulent economic times. That, as I said, is the short answer.

The longer answer is somewhat more complicated. It involves a topsy-turvy journey through private school finances and fundraising. In the course of this little detective story, bloody as they often are, we will end up turning some of the most accepted and commonplace assumptions of the private school world literally on their heads—leading, in brief, to a number of counterintuitive and seemingly improbable claims on our part. For example, we will be defending the highly implausible view that voluntary giving, contrary to what every other private school (and college) claims, actually drives up the cost of tuition at those schools—never lowers it. And the same counterintuitive claim, by the way, will be made as well about endowment income—the universal security blanket of all private schools and even more so of colleges and universities.

At the same time and in the same vein, we will also be pointing out how big and important a role *waste and duplication* play in the management of a private school as well as colleges, and by analogy, companies and government. In other words, we will be taking the highly critical and therefore unwelcome position that wherever you find a well-endowed Kindergarten-through-12th grade (K-12) school or college/university, you will find at the same time a large amount of waste. And if that alone doesn't upset my colleagues at the well-endowed K-12 schools, then the fact that we go on to seriously question many of the most sacred and cherished policies and beliefs of the private school world in the course of this book certainly will.

Private, independent education, one is sad to say, represents less than 1 percent of all the K-12 education in America. It is therefore particularly important, in light of its very small and somewhat fragile place in the much larger world of parochial and public education, that independent, not-for-profit education be examined and re examined as thoroughly as possible—which means, among other things, with a genuinely Cartesian willingness to question the most basic and hallowed assumptions underlying this otherwise very "private" world.

While private schools unequivocally lead America in quality and in their unwavering pursuit of the highest academic standards, problems nevertheless exist, particularly in the financial area. Understanding these problems and addressing the challenges they pose are consequently every bit as important as understanding private education's many successes and achievements. The fact is, if private education is to continue to have a strong future, we must address these serious challenges, many of which stem from outdated ways of operating, without further delay. Private schools, even those that are well endowed and relatively privileged from a financial point of view, are far from immune to the stresses and strains of the larger economy. Years of unbroken success—and overflowing enrollments and budgets—have mistakenly lulled private schools into believing that their own management models are time tested and therefore well positioned for the future.

Unfortunately, appearances, as the saying goes, are often deceiving, and in the case of private schools, the future is far from secure. In fact, the biggest threat to the viability of private schools comes not from the dangers of external events—economic downturns and the like—but from poor management itself. The primary threat to the future of private education, in my view, comes mainly from within the schools themselves and starts with poor management at the top, with school heads and trustees. I can only hope that this story of one school's success in meeting its own financial challenges—by managing itself in a very different fashion from the standard private school model—will help other school communities meet their own challenges and solve their own short- and long-term problems, and hopefully will give all of us a better appreciation of how much effort on everyone's part must go into creating—and more importantly, sustaining—a successful private school.

Finally, I should perhaps make one last observation of a general nature before bringing this introduction to a close. The private school establishment, like any establishment having the pedigree, longevity, and unquestioned success of so many of our private schools, cannot be expected to welcome criticisms directed at its foundations, or at least at some of its most basic operating premises. Moreover, my analysis and investigation of how other private schools operate admittedly comes across as highly critical on more than one occasion. My dictum to "Think Outside the Box" will undoubtedly be viewed by my fellow headmasters and headmistresses as no more than a euphemism for a frontal attack on how they operate—heretofore successfully and with the best of intentions—their respective schools. So be it. I offer no apologies.

In my view, the private school world has too often indulged in self-serving pats on the back and too little Platonic self-examination. Regardless of how my views and opinions might be taken, in the end I simply could find no satisfactory alternative to the straightforward and highly revealing comparative analysis at the heart of this work. If my criticisms and doubts lead to a little more soul-searching and hopefully a lot more honest dialogue and debate—even a little less self-assurance—within the private school world, then I will consider this book a success.

And lastly, as with everything in life, the answers to any question in the final analysis are far less important or even helpful than the process of questioning and exploration itself. It is in this spirit that I offer you this insider's view, however irreverent it might appear at times, of private school management and finances, and of its implications for the wider world of business and government—and quite possibly for our individual lives as well.

PART 1:

A NEW CHAPTER FOR ONE OF AMERICA'S OLDEST PRIVATE SCHOOLS

Kairos: The perfect moment for decision and action.
(Attic Greek)

A TROUBLED SCHOOL GETS A NEW HEADMASTER

I n the spring of 1981, I found myself in the midst of a very unpleasant "tenure fight" at a small college in Purchase, New York, not as a professor, but as both the academic dean of the college and vice president for academic affairs. In my role as chief academic officer, I was responsible for all tenure recommendations to the president of the college and the board of trustees, whose decision, though virtually "pro forma" in nature, served as the final step on the long road to tenure... or termination. Like many small colleges, Manhattanville College in the 1960s found itself overtenured, having several fully tenured or soon to be fully tenured departments. For a small college running huge deficits many years in a row, the situation called for drastic action. In my view, this meant, at a minimum, calling a temporary halt in the seemingly inevitable tenure process.

In seeking a solution, I recommended denying tenure to four wonderfully capable, admirably hardworking, sufficiently published, otherwise fully qualified junior faculty members for a straightforward and perfectly sane reason: each of those departments in question would have become fully tenured, creating a very unhealthy and inflexible situation for a small college that had no plans, much less prospects, for any significant increases in enrollment, at least in the short term. Instead of the usual "tenure or out" policy, I proposed a three-year renewable term for all our faculty until such time that retirements and other factors made tenure advisable. This seemingly painless approach would satisfy everyone, or so I thought, preserving these four wonderful teachers, and their salaries and benefits, with the added incentive to the college of avoiding the appearance of being stuck in an inflexible tenure rut. What initially was supported almost universally by the board of trustees—and indeed, initially at least, by the four teachers in question—soon became a very divisive and legal fight with the faculty union, which saw my approach, however practical in the short run, as an assault on the system of tenure itself. To make a long and complicated story very short, the board relented under pressure from the faculty, and I soon found myself "persona non grata" on campus—and without a job for the following year.

It was during this very trying period that I received one of the strangest and most unexpected calls of my professional career. The caller asked if I wanted to be interviewed for the headmastership at a school called Columbia Grammar and Prep. Not in my wildest dreams had I ever considered being a headmaster, whatever that might entail. No thank you, I politely told the caller, and thought that that would be the last of it. But for the next two or three days, the caller, who was chairing the search committee for Columbia Grammar, assured me in ever more insistent ways that I would be "ideal" for the job, that I would find it quite challenging, interesting, and so on.

And so it was, in the spring of 1981, when I was least wanted at Manhattanville College, that I finally agreed to pay Columbia Grammar a brief visit. After all, I thought, the school was located on the Upper West Side of Manhattan where, in fact, I often found myself for purely social and cultural reasons. It was also near my old alma mater, Columbia University, where I did my Ph.D. work in philosophy some 15 years earlier.

When I walked in the door of Columbia Grammar and Prep on that beautiful day in April of 1981, I was shocked, to put it mildly, to find something close to bedlam in the front hallway. I had not anticipated seeing some 400 students crowded into a small building, with boys and girls of all ages studying on the stairs. I remember being overwhelmed by the various aromas, of the food from the cafeteria on the left, of the sweaty bodies from the gym on the right, and of the powerful chlorine from the pool straight ahead. And I couldn't help but notice the stained ceiling tiles above my head and the chipped and discolored floor tiles under my feet. The whole scene seemed straight out of the classic film *Blackboard Jungle*, though with happy faces in place of the angry ones in the Hollywood version.

The contrast with the serene campus of Manhattanville College could not have been greater. My office at the college was large enough to house two secretaries, two assistants, a large dog I would often bring to work, and all sorts of carpets, sofas, conference tables, and other paraphernalia associated with being a college dean. It's not that we all had that much to do on a typical day at a small liberal arts college that was seriously under-enrolled. So to walk into this noisy and smoke-filled private school building, with children of all ages seemingly moving at random in all directions, my first instinct was to turn around and run (Yes, in 1981 students and faculty were allowed to smoke in school!). This was my first experience with a private school, having gone through public schools myself, and I thought right then and there that it would also be my last.

Just as I was ready to turn around and make a run for it, a young girl, a seventh grader named Karina, came racing through the bedlam and literally tackled me chest high. She then whirled me around in front of a crowd of cheering students and loudly pronounced, "It's the new headmaster—we love you!" All this was apparently in response to a notice that had been recently posted to the effect that a candidate for the headmaster's position would be visiting that day—the word "candidate" being conveniently overlooked by Karina and her classmates, who nonchalantly and happily assumed that the year-long search for this new headmaster-type had come to an end with me. In any event, Karina then dragged me upstairs to the headmaster's office, where one of my more interesting and rewarding educational experiences began to unfold.

So began my introduction to Columbia Grammar and Prep School.

Virtually every aspect of this first day's visit offered some sort of puzzle or surprise. While the building was dilapidated, overcrowded, dirty, and disorganized, I felt a spirit of excitement, intensity, and commitment on the part of teachers—a grassroots concern with real educational issues that seemed so refreshing when compared to the stale and stereotypical debates at college faculty meetings where medical benefits and parking spaces were always high on the agenda. I also found it surprisingly refreshing being around so many young people. Columbia Grammar offered that feeling to the nth degree, not only because everyone was on top of everybody, but also because the school went from kindergarten through high school.

At the meeting they had called to have the faculty interview me, I found extremely intelligent, highly cultured, and thoughtful teachers who clearly had a sophistication that rivaled any college faculty with whom I had ever worked. The headmaster, who was retiring after 25 years, seemed warm and sensible, otherwise transcending his office decor with its fake leather recliner, horse lamp, and old pine panelling. I felt surprisingly energized and somewhat intrigued walking through the halls, visiting classrooms, talking to teachers, and basically getting a feel for this very unusual environment. Though not at all what I had expected, it was a pleasant and invigorating experience. But, frankly, none of this translated into any serious interest in considering the job, whatever was ultimately involved in being a headmaster.

Nonetheless, I will admit to having developed a very warm feeling for the school by the time I walked around the corner to a Central Park West apartment where members of the board had organized a reception/interview for me. Here again, I was in for a surprise. One of the first trustees I met was Omus Hirshbein, then the long-standing director of the 92nd Street Y concert series. I had season tickets to the concert series for the prior two years and often had heard Omus introduce in his uniquely appealing way any number of world class performers or talk with contagious excitement about future events. With this type of sophistication on the board, I thought something compelling must be going on at Columbia Grammar and Prep. I met book publishers, journalists, prominent real estate people, and other sophisticated types, giving me a taste of the high end of New York arts and letters and business community.

But the icing on the cake in terms of surprise and appeal was meeting an actress I had greatly admired when I was a student in Paris in the early 1960s—Barbara Barrie, who had won the Best Actress award at the Cannes Film Festival in 1962 for her breathtaking—and heartbreaking—role in the film *One Potato, Two Potato*. The story involved an interracial marriage and the negative reaction of a small Southern town, the subsequent loss of a daughter, and other themes having to do with the powerful racism of the South in the 1950s. While the film was rarely, if at all, shown in the United States, it was a major hit in Europe, and everyone who saw the movie fell in love with Barbara Barrie and her extraordinary performance. And here she was, warmly greeting me as a member of the board and as a parent of two children enrolled at the school. Although this did not dispel my skepticism about the prospect of being headmaster, it did at least open me to the idea that I should think about this possibility a little further.

However, it was not until a month or so later, while visiting my older sister in Richmond, Virginia, that the prospect of becoming the next headmaster of Columbia Grammar and Prep School began to make some real sense for me. Although the school had offered me the job a few days after my visit and I had politely declined, the chairman of the board continued to call me, even somehow tracing me to Richmond, where my sister overheard one of the conversations I was having with him. After I had again politely declined the offer and had hung up the phone, my sister pressed me for an explanation. When I told her about this odd job offer and even odder school in New York City, her first reaction was to say, "This is perfect for you." I had never known my sister to be anything but intuitively correct about life in general but particularly about *my life*, especially anything to do with my best interests. Hence, I started thinking very seriously about the strange prospect of becoming a headmaster, still quite uncertain as to what such a job would ultimately entail.

When I returned to New York, the school offered me a five-year contract, which I again declined, but I agreed on the basis of a handshake to work one year to see how I might do at this job for which I had no direct qualifications, no relevant experience (as far as I could tell), and except for my sister's encouragement, no real interest in running this obviously run-down little private school, somewhat hidden away on the Upper West Side.

While it was certainly true that I personally had never heard of the school before receiving that surprising phone call in the spring of 1981, it isn't entirely fair or accurate on my part to imply that the world at large was unfamiliar with this school that stretched back over the centuries. This wasn't just another private school in Manhattan on the periphery of its more illustrious neighbors on the East Side, but the oldest non-sectarian private school in the United States. Its history was impressive, reaching back before the Revolutionary War. Good old King George II had founded King's College in New York in 1754, and a decade later in 1764, The Grammar School of King's College was established to prepare the college's future students in the fields of English, Greek, and Latin grammar. After the Revolutionary War came the name change: King's College became Columbia College, and its preparatory school became The Grammar School of Columbia College. The all-boys grammar school functioned for a century under the direct auspices of the college, with such notables among its student body as Herman Melville and his older brother, Gansevoort. Then in 1864, the trustees of Columbia College terminated their relationship with the Grammar School and the school became a private institution. Having existed in several locations over the centuries, it moved to its present location on the Upper West Side of Manhattan in 1907.

At that time, the school was still very much among the elite private schools in the city. In fact, one of my favorite old photographs from that period shows the school community gathered for what would become our present day "spring benefit" with the ladies in beautiful gowns and the men in elegant tuxedos at the Waldorf Astoria. In the photo, George Rupert, head of the Rupert Brewery family, is seated on the dais next to John Vernon Bouvier, Jackie Kennedy's grandfather, and these two lions of New York City life and culture are identified respectively as President and Vice-President of the Board of Trustees. This somewhat grand period continued right through the 1950s before the school began to experience, along with all of New York City, a slow but steady decline—ultimately into insolvency for both the city and the school at precisely the same moment in the late 1970s. Along the way, however, Columbia Grammar continued to attract some of the finest students and families in the city, to name only a few: Lorenz Hart of Rodgers and Hart fame; Richard Adler of *Damn Yankees*; Murray Gell-Mann, who won the 1969 Nobel Prize in physics; and William Kapell, Gary Graffman, and Byron Janis—America's three most promising pianists of the 1950s and 1960s. Nevertheless, the general decline of New York City took its toll on Columbia Grammar and Prep, along with dozens of other private schools and indeed the public school system most of all. It was at this low and inauspicious point that I became the school's thirteenth headmaster.

And so began this latest chapter—and to my mind, perhaps the most interesting of all—in the long history of one of America's oldest private schools.

CONGRATULATIONS, YOU'RE INSOLVENT

It is hard to know where to begin describing the school I inherited in the fall of 1981. Many of the surprises I encountered were due to my own lack of experience. While I had asked about finances as well as other obvious areas such as enrollment, the academic program, and staffing, I soon realized that the somewhat vague and general answers from the search committee members and trustees didn't begin to reveal the monumental problems I now faced.

The biggest surprise of my first trustee meeting was the revelation that the school was bankrupt, or technically speaking, insolvent. What this meant in actual terms was that the school had run up a cumulative deficit of nearly $700,000 against an annual budget of $1.1 million. Schools, of course, have a number of hidden pockets to borrow from during times of crisis or hardship—endowment funds, capital reserves, and pre-paid tuition are the three most readily available and common sources of emergency borrowing. Unfortunately, Columbia Grammar had depleted all its hidden pockets, meager as they were to begin with, by the time I attended that first trustee meeting.

A quick analysis carried out with my business officer, who was hired just three or four months prior to my arrival—and who is still very happily by my side today—indicated that we would run out of cash by the following May, meaning that we couldn't pay faculty for the final two months of the year, not to mention the three summer months for those who were on a 12-month payroll plan. And to top it off, the departing headmaster, in a gesture of good will, had increased faculty and staff salaries by 11.5 percent for the 1981-1982 school year, while the school for its part had committed itself to a large severance package for my predecessor, whether appropriate or not I cannot say, but which had to come directly from the operating budget since there was no other source for these extra funds!

So how was the school going to raise the desperately needed revenue to survive? There are only a few basic ways to do so for a private school. The first and foremost, of course, is through tuition income, and our tuition had crept downwards over the years to be among the lowest in New York City, especially during the previous five years when enrollments were declining. Tuition increases remained at a minimum, in the board's wise judgment, as a way to keep attrition as low as possible. The thinking was that the better the bargain, so to speak, the more likely parents were to stay in the school or possibly be attracted to Columbia Grammar and Prep from other schools. The board was 100 percent convinced that any tuition increase beyond cost of living would drive enough families out of the school to cause us to close our doors. The prevailing notion from the trustees' point of view and shared by faculty and staff was that we were a "blue collar" Upper West Side school, private in one sense, but very public in the more relevant sense of catering to families who would otherwise be in public schools had the public school system not deteriorated both academically and from a perspective of safety. But our no-frills Freddie Laker (the flamboyant precursor to today's Jet Blue) formula wasn't working very well in the highly competitive private school world.

After tuition income, the second most common way that schools raise money is through voluntary giving, which had come virtually to a halt at Columbia Grammar and Prep, given its many problems—false starts with capital campaigns that went nowhere, and new building projects that never got off the ground. I came to realize just how bleak this situation was in my first few days in office. On the wall I had noticed a framed $25 check with the inscription that it was the first $25 toward the "Columbia Grammar and Prep School Endowment." When I asked our bookkeeper how much money we had in the endowment, he told me that as far as he could determine, it was zero. I replied that there must be at least $25, because here was the cancelled check itself! But the sad reality was that the endowment fund was nonexistent, along with every other fund that might represent some help for an operating budget in desperate need.

A third obvious way to raise money is to borrow it. The problem here was that the school had lost its credit rating by 1981. Given our circumstances, we could not borrow even a dollar from our local bank, then Manufacturers Hanover Trust. The situation was critical.

As it turned out, the ensuing discussion about our fiscal crisis wasn't at all "news" to the board members. Clearly, similar discussions had taken place the prior spring, but the incoming headmaster—I—had been kept in the dark. The board had conveniently "forgotten" to mention during my various interviews that they were seriously contemplating putting the entire lower school, which was housed in four adjacent brownstones on West 94th Street, *up for sale*! The thought was to use the proceeds to pay off the debts and to preserve a 7-12 upper division or at minimum a 9-12 upper division with some reasonable hope for steady enrollment and a balanced budget for the near future.

Indeed, most of this board meeting was taken up with discussion about placing the four brownstones, and a fifth one the school owned but had not yet refurbished, on the market for the then-unheard-of sum of $3.5 million, or roughly $700,000 a brownstone. This was at a time when brownstones were selling for $50,000 on West 94th Street. On the one hand, I was shocked that the school, or at least half of it, was being put up for sale, and on the other I was heartened that it was a pipe dream, given the amount the board wanted for the five brownstones. Since I believed they couldn't raise that amount, no matter how long they tried, that effort would give me the much needed time to analyze the needs of the school and come up with a strategic plan to secure its future.

My recommendation was that the board give me, the new headmaster, six months to assess the situation with the understanding that early in the spring the whole matter would be reconsidered. This was agreed upon, and this was the way I gingerly started my first year, which I thought at the time would be my only year.

As bad as our financial situation was, however, many other problems needed more immediate attention. The physical plant, for one, was an obvious area of concern. While the main school building, established in 1907, was solid, workable, and even potentially attractive, it was in a state of almost total disrepair. Not only were the tiles coming up at the edges in the hallway floors and the cafeteria, but the stair treads were worn, the florescent lighting was unattractive, and the hallways were coated with many layers of poor paint jobs—all of which gave the school an overall appearance of decline and neglect. It was clear to prospective parents as well as this new headmaster that the building had not received any serious care or attention for years.

Behind this facade, however, were even more serious issues, even dangerous ones. The wiring was faulty, to the point where plugging in a toaster was sufficient cause for a short or an overload, and some of the toilets and spigots in the building were producing water with a yellow-green tint—though, fortunately for the children, the water fountains were spared this contamination! Indeed, to this day, I have in my closet a three-foot piece of piping with all of the corroded materials inside as a reminder of the long road we've traveled since those early days when we faced a physical plant in dire need of total renovation.

MIKE MIKRUT—IN THE NICK OF TIME!

With only the barest budget for maintenance and nothing at all for improvement, it was hard to know where to begin. Walking home from school one afternoon during my second month, while contemplating the dilemma we faced, I wanted to light up my pipe but discovered that I had no matches in my pocket. Walking along on that sunny day, I found a pack of matches virtually untouched on the sidewalk just a few blocks from the school. When I opened it up to light my pipe, I noticed an ad on the inside of the matches. It said: "Do you need a maintenance man? Call Triple A Employment on 42nd Street."

Being superstitious, in spite of my years of rational training as a philosophy professor, I thought this indeed was a good omen, a moment of serendipity I will always remember. The next day I called a gentleman at Triple A Employment Agency and asked if he had anyone resembling my own father, someone who could do plumbing, electrical work, carpentry, tile work, in brief everything one needed to repair, build, and refinish from top to bottom any type of home or building. I said I was looking for someone who had perhaps recently gotten off a boat from Europe or some other place, as had my father at the turn of the Twentieth Century. I was looking for someone with the same work ethic as my father, a man untouched by any notion of labor unions, long breaks, shoddy work, and cutting corners. To my utter surprise and without hesitation, he replied, "I have just the man you need," and indeed he did.

The next morning I met Mike Mikrut, the spitting image of my father in every regard, from his sense of responsibility toward hard work to the ability to perform all his duties at the level of a master craftsman. We settled on a modest salary, and I said, "If you turn out to be anything like my father, I will double your salary in three months." To be exact, it took less than a week to see that Mike was every bit a dream come true, and his salary was happily doubled on the spot! Among other improvements in the quality of our lives, we could now enjoy clean water from all the taps in the brownstones and would not have to worry any longer about the lights going dark just because a coffee pot had been plugged in by an unsuspecting teacher. Call it what you will—a miracle, serendipity, or just plain luck—that book of matches will always be for me a magic moment, and the beginning of the story of Columbia Grammar and Prep's renewal.

Hirschel Abelson and
Dr. Soghoian

Dr. Soghoian
with
Carl Morse
and David
Steinmann

Jerry Heymann and Dr. Soghoian

Richard and Stephanie Soghoian

Dr. Soghoian with Mary and Peter Kalikow

Columbia Grammar School in the early 1900s

The proposed
middle school atop
36 West 93rd Street

Dr. Soghoian and
Dr. Larry Howard

Neil Crespi and Andrew Zaro with
Dr. Soghoian

Dr. Soghoian and Mike Mikrut

Photography: Charles Abbott, Alida Durham Clemans, Philip Greenberg, Elaine Kingman, Julie Lam, Blanca Millan, Robin Platzer-Judson, Joan Tedeschi, Marvin Terban, Sara Ziff
Historical photographs courtesy of Columbia Grammar and Preparatory School archives.

A NEW ENGLAND TOWN COUNCIL

While finding Mike was an optimistic first step, many seemingly insurmountable problems remained: The school's finances threatened our very existence, enrollment had to be increased significantly, additional classrooms and labs for both science and art had to be found, specialists in math and reading had to be hired, the student/teacher ratio had to be reduced if quality was to be improved, and the overall question of morale among both parents and teachers had to be addressed. With little time to spare, I had to think in bold terms and as far outside the box as I could, since "business as usual" meant closing our doors for good.

By the end of the fall term, I had come to a couple of firm conclusions. In spite of the fact that our most severe enrollment decline was in the lower divisions, especially kindergarten, I decided that we needed to keep the lower school open. I felt that, more than anything, a strong lower school was the key to our long-term viability. Why? Because kindergarten parents bring the most excitement and deepest commitment of any parents to a school. These families represent a critical income stream that you can count on and plan around for years to come. A strong and happy pool of early childhood parents also constitutes the best publicity for attracting new children and families, especially in New York City where the best way to share insights about which schools are worth applying to is by word of mouth.

Secondly, I came to the even stronger conclusion that we needed to increase tuition to a level that would allow us to move forward with more competitive hiring, more enriched programs, additional reading and math specialists, refurbished buildings, and so on. While fundraising would help us accomplish all these goals, the only short-term answer lay in a significant increase in tuition. I proposed to the board, to its utter consternation and disbelief, that we should raise tuition 17.50 percent for the 1982-1983 school year. Since the average increase among private schools in New York City at that time in the early 1980s hovered around 4 percent a year, the board was convinced that such a large increase would cause our enrollment to plummet and that no new families would be attracted to our school. In brief, such a large increase would spell the end of Columbia Grammar and Prep!

To deal with the issue head-on, I decided to call a New England town council-type meeting in our little gym. I stood on an elevated platform in the middle of the gym surrounded by approximately 250 anxious parents, with many more jammed in the hallway leading all the way up the stairs to the front door. The only thing I could offer them, besides the shocking proposal that we raise tuition 17.50 percent, was a glass (actually a paper cup) of cheap white wine, which they could grab from each of the four corners of the gym from large gallon jugs. We started the two-hour evening talking about the many problems the school faced at the present time and the many opportunities we could have over the coming years to create one of the finest little schools in New York City—with their critical financial help.

I then outlined my goals for the school. I wanted to put two teachers in each of the lower school classes instead of one with an assistant. I wanted to hire specialists, reading and math in particular, develop new programs, introduce computers (a relatively novel idea in 1982), and thoroughly re-furbish the school—from the many cosmetic needs we faced to the under-lying structural problems that included plumbing, electrical, new roofs, and so forth. I also insisted on something we couldn't avoid, a 20 percent deposit up front by April 5th for all continuing families—heretofore, the school had required only a small deposit, which was rarely enforced or collected. As embarrassing and risky as it was to discuss, I told the parents that the school was literally going to run out of money by mid May at the latest without that down payment on next year's tuition. In brief, I counted on a leap of faith on the part of parents, in addition to their contributions, something that the board thought would definitely not materialize in ei-ther case. And after two hours of debate, which was heated and raucous at times, I concluded the meeting with the promise that families who stayed would not only end up with a wonderful education for their children but would be part of an exciting period of growth and renewal for this very special school. And I promised one more thing: *I would stay if they would stay—and pay for a better future for their children.*

While this is not the end of the story, to paraphrase Churchill, "It's not even the beginning of the end, but it's the end of the beginning." In the spring of 1982, we had the first increase in enrollment that the school had had in five years, and we lost only one family through attrition. So much for doing what the board had said couldn't be done—and against all rational expectations, we started off September 1982 with much energy and hope for a long-awaited renewal.

RUN FOR FUNDS

Fundraising is built into the fabric of private education in New York City. Annual funds, capital campaigns, endowment funds, spring benefits, phonathons, and the ubiquitous fundraising brochures generated by development offices fill up the calendar in any independent school. Columbia Grammar and Prep was perhaps the lone exception in 1981. It had the unfortunate record of three successive failed capital campaigns for buildings that got designed but never built, for land that was hoped for but never purchased, and for dreams that were impressively described in brochures but ultimately were abandoned for one reason or another.

To be specific, the school's annual fund, including money raised through special events such as the spring benefit, totalled less than $15,000 in 1980-1981, the year before I arrived. Considering the fact that the three-person development office—director, assistant director, and secretary—were making over $100,000 total (a substantial sum in those days), the fundraising formula at Columbia Grammar and Prep was a clear-cut losing proposition.

One of my many "first tasks" as headmaster was to figure out some way to raise voluntary giving to an acceptable level. The annual fund was a year-long effort, and the best I could do was to formulate some literature and a theme early in the fall. But the payoff surely wouldn't be until late in the spring. A capital campaign was an even longer-term mission, and to be truthful I had yet to formulate our long-term plans, since it was only my second month in the school. What could we do, I wondered, to come up with some type of enjoyable fundraiser that had an air of immediacy or even urgency about it? Putting these ingredients together, the thought occurred to me that I would run the New York City Marathon and get pledges per mile either for our annual fund or for a specific goal such as scholarships for needy students. We settled on the latter theme, and I made preparations, usually between 6:00 and 7:00 in the morning in Central Park and after school many days of the week, to get my body in shape for this 26-mile event.

Actually, I had been preparing for the New York City Marathon for a year, while I was still dean at Manhattanville College. It all began one hot, humid day when I decided at the last moment to drive into Manhattan from Westchester to watch the Marathon from Central Park. I parked my car on 72nd Street across from a Cakemasters, which was a franchise bakery in New York City in those days, and bought a sweet roll and a cup of coffee before sauntering into Central Park for what I thought would be a very casual and mildly interesting experience of watching the runners near the end of the race.

When I made it to the 25-mile mark in Central Park, I sat at the curb, leaning my back against a light pole, and did what I regularly did in those days: smoked a cigarette while enjoying my coffee and sweet roll. It was a picture far removed from what you would associate with a marathon runner or even a decent athlete, which I was back in high school and even in college, playing a variety of sports and continuing with mild-mannered athletics such as tennis, though not actually keeping in very good shape.

Such was my state of mind and physical condition that year before I had yet to hear the name of Columbia Grammar and Prep. Leaning there against the light pole in the fall of 1980, in what can be described as casual interest bordering on mild curiosity and waiting for the first runner, I experienced one of the true surprises of my life. I can remember distinctly holding an unfiltered Camel cigarette half-smoked in one hand and a cup of coffee in the other when Bill Rodgers came up the slight hill leading to the 25-mile mark and the light pole where I was idling and more or less indifferently seated. I saw him flowing up that hill toward me with the sweat glistening on his body and with a combination of power and gracefulness that only comes from months of hard work and determination. This was a pure instance of an athlete as a role model. Watching him literally sent a wave of electricity through my body—much to my astonishment and surprise, and in an instant Bill Rodgers became my role model—and hence my instantaneous resolve to become an athlete once again. Perhaps the experience tapped into my long dormant memories of high school athletics and my long-passed competitiveness in a number of sports—or more simply, an early New Year's resolution to stop smoking and get myself into respectable shape once again. Whatever the explanation, it was one of those experiences that literally changed my perspective from that day forward.

I remember putting out the cigarette, pouring out the coffee on the grass, and telling myself after Bill Rodgers had passed that the following year I would run by this very spot. While I suppose I have had other such "conversions" in my life that were conveniently forgotten sometime later, this one turned out to be quite real. I started training, or at least running, the next day and hardly missed a day until that fall of 1981 when I ran the New York City Marathon to raise money for Columbia Grammar and Prep School. Based on the prospect that I would run the Marathon, we came up with a full-fledged campaign, which we ended up calling the "Run for Funds." The campaign—in spite of our "amateur status" as fundraisers—rapidly took on a life of its own, building into great excitement, enthusiasm, and best of all, a growing momentum generated almost exclusively by the students themselves who ended up getting all the pledges per mile from parents, friends, and neighbors during the coming weeks. All I had to do was run—and hopefully complete—the New York City Marathon in 1981.

The night before the Marathon, students and parents joined me for a big pasta dinner in our little gym—the traditional carbohydrate loading pre-marathon meal. Various people made speeches in the hopes that I could complete this 26-mile 345-yard great race. It was a wonderful evening of fun and enthusiasm. Plans were hatched to have a large crowd at the 25-mile mark to acknowledge, even commemorate, the spot where I had had my little inspiration to quit smoking cigarettes and to take up running.

The race took place on a beautiful sunny day in 1981, and somewhere between 300 and 400 parents and children had indeed gathered at the 25-mile mark near that now-famous light pole to greet me with a boldly lettered banner—Columbia Grammar & Prep—strung across the East Side Drive about 30 feet off the ground. (The Parks Department claimed that it was the only such banner that had ever been allowed by a private group, but the exception had been made in light of the worthy goal involved.) But nearing the 24-mile mark, I suffered horrible fatigue and cramps and wondered how I could possibly make it another two-plus miles. At the very least, I needed to make it to the 25-mile mark where everyone was waiting.

Then about half a mile before that spot, my leg cramps turned into an incredible Charley horse or weird muscle bump in my right thigh. It was the size of a grapefruit and stopped me in my tracks. Much to my embarrassment and shock, one of the many policemen lined up to control the very large crowds in the park rushed to my assistance and started massaging the grapefruit-sized bulge with his hands. To my disbelief, after about 10 minutes, the bulge subsided—due I suppose to his ministrations—and with his encouragement (he ran along with me for about 20 paces), I hobbled along until I passed under the banner to the cheers of hundreds of children and parents, cameras flashing, to a true hero's welcome.

Somehow, I managed to make it to the finish line—in 3 hours 52 minutes. We raised $25,000 that day, double what the annual fund was raising in a year. A charitable foundation generously matched the $25,000, and we were off and running, to use a pun, toward an $85,000 year for scholarships. It was a godsend for an insolvent school trying to get back on its feet.

The Associated Press picked up the story from one of the local papers about our marathon "Run for Funds," and the next thing I knew, heads of private schools were calling me with congratulations from as far away as California, asking if they could borrow the idea for their own fundraising goals. I was only too happy to see the idea spread, as long as I did not have to do the running! But my advice to anyone who might want to brave the "Run for Funds" approach for their school—or any other cause—is not to cheat Mother Nature; give the marathon the respect it deserves by training thoroughly for a 26-mile race. The marathon is a stern taskmaster. You can't cut corners (I had given up cigarettes, but not my favorite pipe) when you are training for a marathon, and while I had trained with some seriousness relative to the life of a non-runner, I realized that I had not properly prepared for the demands of this race.

The following year I ran the Marathon again with the same "Run for Funds" effort, though it generated only $15,000 the second year. Again the charitable foundation matched it, giving us a pot of money totaling over $100,000 in the endowment for student scholarships—not much by New York City private school standards, but enough to bolster our confidence about the future. And, very happily, two years later, this foundation gave us another grant of $35,000 when we held a similar, but even larger "Run For Funds" by inviting a group of parents to join me in the 26-mile effort, in which all but one finished. So far then, the story is nothing but positive and full of morale-boosting efforts on all sides—not to mention, a growing endowment.

GIUSEPPE AND THE VIRGIN MARY

Having developed a supportive and generous relationship with this prominent foundation, I took the next ambitious step of applying for a more traditional foundation grant. I requested $50,000 to help us complete our new high school building in 1984, which was under construction and on a very tight budget.

The foundation director called me for the standard face-to-face interview, but instead of quizzing me on the high school project, which I had anticipated, he surprised me by launching into a stern lecture on the importance of annual giving. He and the trustees of the foundation had noticed that annual giving had steadily decreased over the last three years—a dangerous sign that the school was in trouble and that the parent body did not have confidence in my leadership. Did I not know, he said, that a growing annual fund was *the* single most important criterion used by the foundation in assessing the health and long-term prospects of a given school?

In turn, I proudly pointed out to him that total giving had gone up each of the past three years, even though "annual giving" as such had gone down—but purposefully so. I naively explained to him that I had resolved to operate our school on tuition alone, and consequently, was fazing out the annual fund. I tried my best to defend this point of view, but it was difficult to articulate in those early years—something along the lines that I thought the best way to operate a school was to use "annual giving," or overall voluntary giving for the year, exclusively for capital improvements, growth, etc. and tuition, on the other hand, for operations only.

To make a long story short, there was simply no way that I could convince him that what we were trying to do—slowly but deliberately eliminate annual giving from our operating needs—was reasonable or in any way fiscally sound. The well-intentioned director, a former head of school himself, I might add, would simply not hear of it. In short, his answer to our grant proposal was an emphatic "no" with an invitation to re-submit when and only if we had reversed the decline in our annual giving—and indeed, returned to our senses! His parting words were to the effect that the annual fund was the single most important standard of a "successful" private school and that I would do myself, and more importantly my school, a service by concentrating on policies that were both time tested and with proven merit—and not on approaches that would inevitably perpetuate, or at least, exacerbate the financial problems I had inherited in the first place. What was also quite clear to him was that this newly minted headmaster did not know what he was doing, and that this particular foundation would have no further part to play in his short-sighted schemes.

I certainly did not have any concrete evidence either to prove my point or disprove his, much less the confidence or experience needed to question him at that early and very tentative stage in my thinking. Though intuitively or instinctively I felt that I was on the right track, Columbia Grammar was still struggling financially, and I was understandably in no position to argue the point with any credibility. And to make matters worse, the foundation director was not the only source for my own increasing doubts and second-guessing, as Columbia Grammar struggled to stay alive in those difficult early years. After all, many of the other well-to-do and established private schools were shining rebuttals to my fledgling approach. The successful ones had growing annual funds and the less than successful ones were trying to copy their more fortunate peers. All the evidence seemed to indicate that the conventional model was the way to go. Common sense seemed to confirm conventional wisdom at every turn: Annual funds quite obviously constituted a net plus for any school's financial needs. Voluntary gifts pouring in each year from parents and alumni directly enhanced a school's operating budget—providing more scholarships, higher faculty salaries and benefits, more enriched and better funded academic programs, and so on and so forth—in short, more money to operate the school. *What could possibly be wrong with that?*

Indeed, the annual fund was then and remains today such a rock-solid part of the world of private school fundraising that any departure from this norm had to raise doubts in any rational person's mind—including my own, to be honest! Nevertheless, against my growing doubts and in the face of ever-growing financial pressures, I remained committed to operating the school on tuition alone—or, at least, trying to do so. After all, I hardly had a choice in those early years. At the same time, it was slowly becoming clearer to me that even if I had had a choice at that time, I would have remained skeptical of the conventional model of tuition plus annual giving as the best way to run a school—at least in the long run. It seemed to me, even in the midst of extreme financial need, that a dependency on ever larger annual funds to operate a school was a questionable approach to take, one that was based more on custom and unexamined habit than sound fiscal policy. In brief, the foundations of a new approach to managing our school, along with a growing confidence that we could manage to operate our school on tuition alone was beginning—slowly, but surely—to take shape in my mind. If only I could buy enough time to give it a chance to succeed!

In those early years, on many occasions, I tried talking about—and of course questioning—the concept of annual giving with various colleagues who ran private schools in the city. I got nowhere, to put it mildly. Either I was pulling their legs, they would assume, or simply covering up the embarrassing fact that I couldn't generate a growing annual fund myself, something the "Run for Funds" foundation had already accused me of failing to do! Annual funds were here to stay, whether I liked it or not!

Private schools—and even more so, private colleges—take it for granted that annual giving combined with endowment income should rightfully cover a substantial portion of the academic year's operating budget. One college, in fact, to my enormous amusement, actually celebrates the day each year that all funding for operations shifts from tuition to tax-exempt dollars—and appropriately names that day *Mind The Gap Day!* One has to rub one's eyes, but this well-known, reputable, and long-standing college proudly invites alumni and parents to the campus to join up with faculty and students to have something akin to an old-fashioned May Day celebration, all in the name of deficit spending!

Whenever I think too hard about the stubbornly entrenched and sacrosanct role that annual giving played and continues to play in the minds and hearts of school heads everywhere, I am reminded of an incident from my youthful days as a student abroad. It occurred while I was on an English-Speaking Union scholarship to study at the University of Edinburgh. The year was taken up more with travel than study, as such, and during this time I found myself visiting a friend who was similarly "studying" in Rome that year.

My friend introduced me to the delights of a small, very cheap Italian restaurant in a working class section of Rome filled with every walk of Roman life other than students and the rich. Workers of all stripes ate there every evening, and the conversations were invariably about politics and always heated and loud.

In the early 1960s, in Rome, as anyone old enough to recall knows, there was seemingly a change in Italian government—in Rome as well as nationally—every other week. Political banners perpetually hung from apartment buildings and businesses, with extravagant graffiti everywhere, and the Communist and Socialist parties dominating the headlines.

Well, to get to the point of this story, we were often served by a middle-aged waiter named Giuseppe, who loved to talk both about religion and politics, much to my delight as a philosophy major who shared a similar passion. As it became clear in our conversations, Giuseppe was highly critical of the Catholic Church, particularly the Pope and any notion that he might be "infallible," along with any of the other "nonsense" and "fairy tale stories" offered by the Church of Rome. It was all just a grand scheme to take advantage of the poor and weak. With its money, riches, land, and slavery, the Catholic Church was no less than what Karl Marx had showed all religion to be: "the opiate of the masses." Giuseppe would have nothing to do with any of it, but most especially the Catholic Church, for the obvious reason(s) that he and his fellow Italians were most personally affected by its influence.

I found this all quite fascinating, particularly when Giuseppe proudly announced that he was a member of the Communist Party. For a young man who grew up in the South in the 1940s and 1950s, running across a real, live communist was heady business. To the typical Southerner, John

Dillinger posed less danger to society than an honest to goodness communist—and a "card-carrying communist" was at the very top of the list of dangerous characters hidden away in the folds of American society.

Could Giuseppe actually be a "card-carrying communist"? During one of our more animated conversations about politics, I asked Giuseppe if he actually carried a "communist card."

"Of course," he proudly proclaimed in Italian, "of course." At which point, he whipped out his wallet to show us his card. I could not believe my good fortune. Finally, after hearing about "card-carrying communists" throughout my youth, finally, here in Rome, I was to lay my eyes on an actual Communist party membership card.

But as Giuseppe opened his wallet, the first thing my eyes lighted on was an elaborate and brightly colored picture of the Virgin Mary, prominently displayed on the inner front of the wallet.

"Giuseppe," I exclaimed in puzzlement, "what in the world are you doing with that photo of the Virgin Mary? You have been telling us that you don't believe in the Catholic Church, the Pope, any of the saints, and indeed, in religion at all, so how come you have a photo of the Virgin Mary in your wallet?"

Giuseppe looked at me with his own brand of puzzlement and resignation, and simply sighed: "For sure I don't believe in the Pope or the saints, but *the Virgin Mary*, of course!"

So it is that anyone questioning "the institution of annual giving" is likely to incur the wrath of the high priests of private education. It is tantamount, in the final analysis, to religious dogma that is every bit as tenacious and sacrosanct as the role that the Virgin Mary played in Giuseppe's worldview. Certain dogma and customs are to be followed but not questioned—regardless of rational argument and study. Indeed, anyone who dares cast doubt on the virtues of annual funds might well be summarily found guilty of heresy and burned at the stake during the next convention of the National Association of Independent Schools!

It is therefore with a healthy dose of professional caution and with all due respect for my venerable fellow heads that I nevertheless venture forth in the second section of this book, "All Things Financial," with my doubts and questions about this much-loved institution we so innocently and harmlessly call the Annual Fund. And indeed I might well need the blessings of a higher power myself once my colleagues read what I have to say about their favorite fundraising tool.

LET'S MAKE A DEAL

Later that first year came another surprise and one of the biggest shocks of my career. I was called to a meeting with two members of the executive board and the head of the real estate firm that had been hired to sell the school's brownstones. We met in the large, spacious offices of what was then the largest, most successful, and most dominant real estate firm on the Upper West Side. The firm was known for controlling virtually all of the brownstone sales from Lincoln Center up to 96th Street, from Central Park West to Riverside Drive. In that sense, the firm was the natural representative to choose to sell our own five contiguous brownstones. But what I learned at that meeting has left me almost speechless to this day. The four of us—the president of the firm, our two executive board members, and this new headmaster—went into the firm's conference room adjacent to the president of the firm's office and proceeded through the conference room to yet another much smaller, windowless room. If this sounds strange, you are beginning to understand my own sense of suspense and anticipation. What in the world were we doing?

At first I literally couldn't follow the conversation since it had to do with not only selling the five brownstones but selling 5 West 93rd as well, which was the upper school for grades 7-12. The five brownstones located on 94th Street and 5 West 93rd Street formed one large property. Given the zoning allowances at that time in New York City, these six buildings essentially formed a pass-through property with a 75-foot frontage on 93rd Street and approximately 90 feet on West 94th, providing a developer the opportunity to build quite a substantial building, eight to ten stories high, on that site. The conversation then went from the development opportunities on the present school site to a piece of property at 67th and Broadway that was vacant at the time. To make a complicated conversation that I could barely follow short, the plan was to sell the entire school and build a new building on this new site at 67th and Broadway.

On the surface that plan could be viewed as a wonderful future for Columbia Grammar and Prep, and indeed it was presented to me as some

47

sort of golden opportunity. But some obvious questions immediately arose. Would the school have to close for an extended period of time? The answer to this question was yes. When was the school going to be sold and for how much? When was the new construction to begin and for how much? When was the new school going to start and for what grades? Where was the money to come from for this expensive new building that far exceeded any potential proceeds from the old? The answers to those many questions were less clear.

After two hours of discussion and questions, mainly on my part, I gleaned from the various responses and comments that the two executive board members, both of whom were in real estate, were going to receive a fairly substantial fee on the sale of the school and a similar fee from the purchase of the site at 67th Street and Broadway. If you couple this conflict of interest with an almost cavalier disregard for the future existence of Columbia Grammar, I was left with a disbelief bordering on astonishment. In brief, these two men wanted me to recommend to the entire board, along with them, this risky plan of action, and they indicated that I would be a beneficiary of this fee arrangement as well. The whole proposal seemed to me too preposterous to take seriously, but they made it clear to me that they were more than serious.

To make a long story short, I left that meeting and wrote a 15-page, handwritten, legal-pad letter to the trustees who were the masterminds behind the scheme. The letter said, in brief, that they should resign immediately from the board or face the consequences of my describing to the board at its next meeting what I had just heard in this conference room. After seeing my ultimatum, they surprisingly tendered their resignations to the board president in a brief note and never showed up again at the school or any school board meeting.

Faced with these backroom dealings regarding the very existence of the school, I decided to tackle the problems of governance at Columbia Grammar on a broader scale. The showdown took place at the next trustee meeting, which was held in one of the conference rooms of a major law firm in New York City, a partner of which was the vice president of the board at this time. I sat down with the board and said that I had started as headmaster with a handshake and a salary commitment but had come to realize after half an academic year that the school faced an array of major problems, financial first and foremost, but also low faculty and parent morale, a deteriorating physical plant, inadequate salaries and benefits, and a serious governance problem on top of it all. And that governance problem closely involved the board of trustees.

I presented them with a deal. I would sign the original five-year contract they had offered me and commit myself to finding any and all solutions to the school's myriad problems, but only if the entire executive committee would agree to resign, though they could continue on as regular trustees if they wished. I told them that I was going to go outside and read the paper so that they could take their time and talk about it, and to let me know. If they rejected my offer, there would be no hard feelings, and we could wish each other well as we parted ways. I said it had been a great year for me and I'd done the best I could. Whether or not our relationship would continue was now in their hands.

I spent 55 minutes reading *The New York Times* in a leather easy chair outside the conference room, fully convinced that I was spending my last moments as Headmaster of Columbia Grammar. I therefore was shocked, to put it mildly, when the door opened and one of the trustees came out with a broad smile on his face. He shook my hand and said, "you've got a deal."

So it was that I got to pick a new executive board, a new president of the board, and quite a few new trustees. Some old members resigned from the board under these tense and confrontational circumstances, and others simply left in light of the growing financial pressures facing the school. After all, trustees have a fiduciary responsibility first and foremost, and few trustees wanted to confront the consequences of years of financial neglect and decline on the part of the school. Hence, I now had a clean slate to work with. That turned out to be the easy part.

The more difficult part remained: It would take years, at best, to rebuild the board of trustees. I also realized that, for the time being at least,

I was essentially on my own. That's something that very few incoming headmasters ever experience, because they often inherit a long, successful tradition, money, well-kept buildings, healthy endowments, trustees who are experienced and well established, a bureaucracy underneath them. These headmasters simply step in as caretakers and keep things going with one or two "new projects" on the drawing boards. But the situation at Columbia Grammar was such that following the status quo was simply going to run the school into the ground. For the forseeable future, by necessity, I had to follow my own best judgment and instincts, even if I were totally new to this still-alien world of private schools and K-12 education. There was no more time to spare. Columbia Grammar and Prep was on a respirator, and I had a few precious months left to pump some life into this wonderful but rapidly declining school.

MAKING DREAMS COME TRUE

My ignorance of the way things were normally done—and what I would be told couldn't be done—helped me improve the school in ways large and small from the very beginning and right down through the years.

In one of my first few days as headmaster, I called two gatherings to introduce myself to all the students, one in the morning with all the K-6 children and another in the afternoon with all the 7-12 students, lower and upper schools respectively. I spent some time talking about myself and describing this new headmaster's personality and interests—running, tennis, pocket billiards, classical music, reading—and then asked the somewhat simplistic question, "What would you want me most of all to do that would make your life more fun and enjoyable and successful here at Columbia Grammar? Just imagine I have a magic wand and can make one, but only one, dream come true!"

The little kids almost unanimously and certainly overwhelmingly pleaded for some time in our swimming pool. At the time, Columbia Grammar and Prep, though lacking science labs, libraries, and theaters, was one of only two private schools in Manhattan with its own swimming pool. But the school's policy, I discovered that morning talking to the small children, was to reserve swimming for grades 7-12, culminating in a very competitive swim program for boys and girls in the high school but excluding the younger children except on rare occasions. So I thought to myself, well, we'll try to work out some swim time for the small kids.

When I met with the older kids in the afternoon and asked them the same question, the older kids overwhelmingly pleaded to get out of swimming! The boys hated the experience for a variety of reasons and the girls primarily because their hair ended up wet all day. So the next day I reversed the school's policy and made swimming a central part of the K-6 program and, to great cheers and applause, not to mention gratitude, eliminated the swim requirement for grades 7-12. And instead of one swim teacher per class of older students, I assigned three swim teachers per class for the younger children, giving them a safe and effective introduction to a lifetime of pleasure. To this day the policy remains happily in effect and serves as one of the centerpieces of our lower school program. And it should go without saying that my reputation among the students for being a "pretty cool guy" started with that simple change in policy at the end of my very first week!

The lesson I learned during those first few days of school regarding the swim program was a fairly obvious one: It pays to be both naive and ignorant and ask some very simple questions if you want to find out how habit and custom come to rule one's life in spite of the fact that there are better ways to do things right under one's nose. As Socrates was forever wont to say: *Wisdom comes from knowing that you do not know*—perhaps the best advice ever given to anyone trying to run a school!

Today, as I said, we have one of the strongest early childhood swim programs that produces lifelong accomplished swimmers, trained and introduced to swimming when they are young and can fully enjoy the water and benefit from our quality swim teachers. While all of this seems so obvious and straightforward today, it only came about because we listened to the children themselves. I made up my mind that week to treat this new job of mine as Socrates would, with lots of naive questions based on my ignorance of all things K-12, and to question everything that was being done, from how and why we teach math to kindergartners to why school starts at 8:00 a.m.

THE LEARNING RESOURCE CENTER IS BORN

The swimming solution was oh-so-easy compared to what came next. At my first official board meeting in September of 1981, I received a request from a trustee seated next to me that was both puzzling and intriguing at the same time. The trustee was the mother of two students who had started in Kindergarten at Columbia Grammar, but were now in 9th (the boy) and 11th (the girl) grades. Her son, though admittedly exceptionally bright, according to all of his teachers, had been "evaluated" as learning disabled sometime during the spring term, and, as was the policy in those days, he had been asked to find a "more appropriate school," meaning a school with a weaker academic environment that might accommodate his so-called learning disability.

So there I was at my first board meeting, sitting next to this trustee/mother, when she handed me a handwritten note, just below the level of the table in a somewhat private manner. The brief note expressed two basic thoughts, the first being her best wishes to me for a successful tenure as headmaster and second, a fervent hope that if I accomplished anything during my years as headmaster, it would be first and foremost to find a way to save learning-disabled children. The note concluded by saying that this was her final board meeting and that she was leaving the board in protest over the school's decision to ask her son as well as other "learning disabled" children to leave the school—for no other reason than that they were learning disabled.

What was I to make of all this? On the one hand, I had heard for the first time the stunning news, since no one had bothered to give me a clear financial picture during my various interviews, that the school was insolvent, and on the other hand, I was learning that the school had been irresponsible, perhaps even cold-hearted, in asking this bright child to leave the school solely because he was learning disabled. Insolvency was already a complex enough thought to try to grasp. What, after all, does it mean for a school to be bankrupt? But this new term, "learning disabled," was an altogether new challenge for this new headmaster who, to the best of his recollection, had never heard the term before, or at least never conjoined with the concept "bright." What did it mean, "bright learning disabled student"?

Back in my office the next morning, I was shown a form letter that said in essence that "your child has been judged/determined to be learning disabled... that the school has a college preparatory program which cannot and does not accommodate learning disabilities, and that you need to look for an alternative school for your child for next fall. Best wishes and goodbye," with a clear message, "good riddance" to boot. I recall throwing out the stack of forms. (I regret to this day not saving at least one of these forms for posterity!) You can imagine what impact this kind of terse note with its unsympathetic tone would have on a family, not to mention the child being asked to leave his school and friends for reasons that are barely understood today—"learning disabled"—even by skilled professionals. (The previous headmaster didn't even bother signing the form, but had the entire document with his signature mimeographed!) Not only were such children and their families suddenly confronted with the loss of the private school that they had been a part of, they now had to deal with, perhaps for the first time, the notion that their children were learning disabled, and they had to face the complex anxiety-producing and sometimes futile attempt to find an alternative school.

It is hard to recall the level of difficulty facing anyone dealing with a learning disability back in the early 1980s or before. There was an enormous amount of prejudice and ignorance surrounding the issue of learning disabilities, and children were quite literally stigmatized by the label. Most families wanted their children's "disabilities" kept secret if at all possible, not the least of all because (as at Columbia Grammar back then) they might well be discriminated against by schools and teachers themselves. Today we have the benefit of more than 30 years of the Americans With Disabilities Act, hundreds of educational reforms large and small, dialogues at every level of schooling from elementary to college, and countless discussions on learning disabilities about what can be done, what ought to be done, and what is being done to help a given child at a given stage in his or her education. And prominent public figures (Whoopi Goldberg, Charles Schwab of financial services fame, and Paul Ofalea, founder of Kinko's, among many others) have shared their trials—and successes—in books and public discussions, helping the world understand what we all well know today: Learning disabilities have nothing at all to do with intelligence and ability. On the contrary, among the most intelligent and able of humankind, past and present, are those with "learning disabilities." However, the climate for so-called learning-disabled students was harsh and cold in those early years of my tenure as headmaster. The early stages represented the merest first step in what has been a long and painful and more often than not unsuccessful attempt to support, educate, and treat a learning-disabled child with dignity and fairness.

But, as a new headmaster, or more relevantly a new person to K-12 education, I had not the foggiest notion of what to do for this trustee's very bright, but supposedly learning-disabled son, or any other learning-disabled child for that matter. All I knew was that what we were doing and what every other college preparatory school in New York City was doing, asking learning disabled kids to leave their schools, was ethically and morally wrong—and, as it turned out—*educationally* wrong as well. I had a number of meetings with administrators, faculty, and parents to find some way to try to help learning-disabled children in our school. During these first two years, we hired as many learning specialists as we could to help the classroom teachers provide an extra dimension of support and partial remediation for the learning-disabled child. Other than that, nothing significant developed at first, except for the fact that I made a promise to myself to find a way, at least within our own school, to address this unacceptable failure on the part of schools to give every child, regardless of convenient labels, a quality education.

It wasn't until the beginning of my third year, however, that the first step to a solution presented itself. Over lunch one day, David Steinmann, who was a new trustee as well as a new parent the previous year, had introduced me to Alice Rosenwald, a very generous person from an enormously philanthropic family, whose children were in another private school but who was interested in finding a private school in New York City that would do something particularly innovative in its curriculum. Alice had given a considerable amount of money over the years to the Covenant House in New York City but had been terribly upset and disillusioned when its then-director, Father Ritter, had been asked to step down for inappropriate behavior of some sort. We met over lunch and I discussed a number of ideas I had been researching regarding new approaches to learning, especially for children with different learning styles and needs, many of whom were labeled "learning disabled" or "learning impaired." My goal was to find a way to educate all children within the parameters of a highly demanding college preparatory program, with no diminution in quality, but with the support that would allow a child with special needs to nevertheless succeed, even flourish.

Alice was immediately intrigued by the prospect and asked me point blank and with no hesitation how much money I needed. I remember vividly being taken aback both by her confidence in my ideas, albeit partially formed as they were at that time, and by her ready willingness to back up her enthusiasm with an immediate gift. I replied that I did not know how much money I might need because I didn't know what exactly I might do with it. I suggested I be given a year to investigate the area through literature and visits to schools that claimed to have programs that addressed the needs of learning-disabled students. There were no mainstream schools at the time in New York City with programs to support learning-disabled children, but there were a few schools, Stephen Gaynor, Churchill, and subsequently Winston Prep, that were designed exclusively for learning-disabled students.

So I ended up having to travel to a number of boarding schools that claimed to have programs within the larger program and pieced together a concept for elementary school children that seemed to me sound from an educational point of view—and happily, it appealed to Alice as well. It seemed, on paper at least, to make sense in terms of finally helping learning-disabled children succeed in a mainstream environment. The program essentially involved one-to-one tutoring by a learning specialist once or twice during the school day (more often twice than not) in areas that were presenting the most severe problems for the child. In other words, each child would have a professional learning specialist within the school who would address specific needs in the context of our day-to-day curriculum in a real time context during the school day—all coordinated uniquely for each child with his or her classroom teacher(s).

It might be hard to comprehend today that the overwhelming majority of teachers, administrative colleagues, parents, and trustees were strongly opposed to my starting a program for learning-disabled children within our general population. During the first few years of the program I received what can only be characterized as "hate mail" from many alumni, who claimed that in one fell swoop I had damaged the reputation of their otherwise reputable alma mater. Faculty meetings were uniformly filled with criticism. While our faculty and staff are uniformly supportive today of our our very successful and long-standing efforts to educate learning-disabled students, it was a very different situation in those early years. It is not at all an overstatement to say that a good three quarters of all faculty and staff were anywhere from mildly to strongly opposed to keeping learning-disabled students in our school, much less admitting such students from other schools where they were failing, and most of all against developing a special program to address their special needs.

To give you just one painful example of the anger and hostility that my ideas caused among the faculty, I vividly recall an upper school faculty meeting where I had invited a very thoughtful, experienced and articulate specialist who tutored learning-disabled children in her private practice in New York City. She gave what I considered a fascinating, practical, and highly professional talk about techniques that all teachers can use to help learning-disabled students accommodate their disabilities and thus succeed both in school and in life. Her presentation could not have been more sensitive, thoughtful, and helpful, yet the then chair of the math department, a long-standing and highly respected senior faculty member, rose to say the following, literally: "What we have heard from you during the last hour is pure nonsense. There are only two types of students: bright and dumb. You are simply giving the dumb ones a new name—learning disabled." Such stupidity and prejudice was astoundingly met with a certain degree of applause, and with no protest whatsoever from other faculty, some of whom no doubt must have felt embarrassed by this public show of rigidity and insensitivity, but were disinclined to speak up in the face of so much hostility. Such was the climate regarding learning disabilities and mainstream education back in the early 1980s at Columbia Grammar, and at every other private school in New York City for that matter. (It should be mentioned, by the way, that I waved goodbye to the teacher in question at the end of the school year, along with a half dozen or so of his closest colleagues, creating yet more anger among a faculty and staff overwhelmingly convinced that I was sending our school to the lower depths of academic mediocrity.)

At the same time, I put my job on the line with trustees as well. Not only were the trustees worried, as were the faculty and alumni, about our reputation as a college preparatory program becoming damaged or suspect, but the trustees were worried—and rightly so—about the potentially high costs of this new enterprise. Specialized schools in the city that offered programs for learning-disabled children charged considerably more than mainstream schools for the obvious reason that specialized education of any sort is very labor intensive, the single greatest cost in any school. The one thing that bought me time with both trustees and parents in general was my commitment to have the program stand on its own feet financially, meaning it would be completely self-sufficient. And so, it was without hesitation that Alice Rosenwald wrote a check for $250,000 to underwrite this new program. The learning disabilities program would be separate, but integrated, a program within a program, separate but equal.

We started with two second graders and a third grader who would otherwise have been asked to leave the school the prior spring, and three students from other private schools in New York City, two third graders and a fourth grader, who were being asked to leave because they were "learning disabled" and couldn't manage one or more aspects of the curriculum. I had called six or seven private schools, some of the most prominent in New

York City that spring, and asked if they had any students who matched the general profile of bright but learning disabled who were being asked to leave because they couldn't manage the curriculum. The fourth grader, for example, came from one of the most high-powered college preparatory programs in the city and was described by the director of the lower school as perhaps the single brightest child she had had in her seven years as director of the lower school—but who couldn't write, in spite of the fact that he spoke and read, she said, "at the Ph.D. level."

"Give him to us," I said. "He's perfect."

Another student came to us from a similarly high-powered college preparatory program; he was also described as extremely bright and not only learning disabled but angry and socially a misfit. My lower school admissions director at the time said that I was literally bringing the school to ruin by admitting a child with these kinds of behavior problems, negative attitude toward school, anger about the world, etc. To make a long story short, we took him, and the rest, as they say in sports, is history. He started as a fourth grader—and what a rocky start it was!—but as a senior, he ended up serving as president of the student body, excelled in five AP classes over the course of his junior and senior years, was respected and well liked by teachers and students, went to the University of Michigan as a presidential scholar, studied in China on a grant, graduated with honors, and is now quite successful as a lawyer here in New York City—hardly someone who was destined to single-handedly ruin our school's reputation! The other student who couldn't write ended up graduating from college with honors and today is a successful Wall Streeter. As it turned out, these two were simply the leading edge for what has become over the past 27 years a small army of successful learning-disabled students, who completely—through their own obvious achievements—shattered any and all notions that learning-disabled students cannot excel at the very highest levels. We now count Harvard, Yale, and Princeton, and indeed, every other Ivy college among the impressive list of colleges and universities our LRC (Learning Resource Center) students have attended—and 100 percent, by the way, have gone on to college!

To run the program, which we called the LRC, I had hired a magnificent learning specialist from Pittsburgh who was marrying a gentleman in New York and relocating. Pam Bellermann turned out to be a superb choice and achieved success with all six students, leading us to double the number of students in the program the following year to 12, then to 18, and over the past 27 years we have settled on the number 65 as the workable size for the program at our school.

One other person was critically instrumental in making the LRC a success and that was Mary Kalikow. Peter and Mary Kalikow transferred their older child from Horace Mann into the fifth grade at Columbia Grammar and Prep in 1989 and subsequently moved their younger from Brearley into our third grade, but it was their becoming active parents and supporters that marked another turning point for our school. For her part, Mary took on the formidable task of elevating our program to educate bright learning-disabled students within a challenging college preparatory program to its next level, and that entailed more than anything providing the program with a strong financial base. Managing a complex program such as the LRC within the larger instructional program was already challenging enough, but running it independently of the general operating budget created seemingly intractable problems in the early years. However, Mary was committed to helping me expand this extraordinary program and at the same time to putting it on a permanent and secure financial footing. And as it turned out, she was more than up to the task.

To begin with, Mary asked me what amount of money was needed to secure the LRC far into the future and to provide the program more immediately with the space it needed to expand to 50 students, or approximately 5 percent of our then-projected enrollment. I came up with the ambitious goal of $3 million, beyond our reach, but nevertheless a realistic assessment of what it would take to fund the program properly. "No problem," Mary replied, and off she went, with a degree of energy, determination, and optimism difficult to capture in words.

Mary had a simple—and winning—formula for raising funds. Each week she would invite some wealthy individual or prominent celebrity who might have influence with a foundation to have lunch with me at the 101 Club, a restaurant owned by the Kalikows in their corporate headquarters at 101 Park Avenue. Please don't take this as name-dropping, but simply as a way of giving you some idea of what my weekly experience was like, and indeed some idea of why Mary's fundraising was so successful. One week it would be the head of AIG, who could tap the Starr Foundation's deep resources, or the head of Barnes & Noble, or Sony America, or Sheldon Solow, a developer on the grand scale that Peter Kalikow himself represented; or in the cultural areas, Beverly Sills, who herself was very committed to the education of the learning disabled, or Anne Ford, who chaired the National Foundation for Learning Disabilities, or Princess Yasmin Aga Khan, who had similar interests, and on and on. Virtually every one of these lunch meetings resulted in some kind of support for the LRC, from checks to promising leads.

Mary was also determined to spread the word far and wide about our efforts, however small and tentative at that stage, to bring learning-disabled students into the mainstream of private, independent education, with no diminution of quality or content in the college preparatory program. Mary was also determined to encourage a broader discussion of learning disabilities, a subject that had been kept under wraps for too long by all facets of our society, including the educational establishment. And so, Mary planned an extravaganza at the Plaza Hotel with well over 500 people attending, including reporters from all the newspapers, most prominently of all from *The New York Post*, which was owned by the Kalikows at the time. Twelve LRC students spoke about their unique struggles with learning and the success that they had finally experienced through the LRC. I am not exaggerating when I say that there were very few dry eyes in the house. The $600,000 in donations raised that day were gratefully accepted, but the goodwill created by the LRC students and the indisputable evidence that we were on the right track with the LRC program were the real successes of that extraordinary luncheon at the Plaza. The word was finally getting out that children with learning disabilities deserved our attention and resources every bit as much as the so-called "normal" population, and not simply by specialized schools set apart from the mainstream, but by all schools. I was determined at that point to see that Columbia succeeded where others feared—or simply didn't want—to tread. And here we are, many years later, with a packed house!

The LRC wasn't—and isn't—an easy program to run because it is very labor intensive, therefore quite expensive, time consuming, of course, and sometimes quite complex to operate. But if there is the will, it is worth every ounce of energy that goes into this type of program. The LRC is what every learning-disabled child—and indeed every child—needs as part of receiving the very finest education that he or she deserves. While we started 27 years ago with only six students, more than 400 students have gone through the program here at Columbia Grammar, and all have continued on to the finest colleges and universities in America. Six of the last seven student government presidents have been LRC students, attesting to the fact that students who work to accommodate learning differences are the first to learn problem-solving and people skills, along with their academic development. These non-academic skills and talents are recognized and appreciated by their classmates, hence their success in student government and ultimately in the larger world. Without a doubt, the Learning Resource Center ranks as my proudest achievement here at Columbia Grammar and Prep School.

GUARDIAN ANGELS AND SERENDIPITY: DORIS ROSENBLUM AND COMMUNITY BOARD 7

Rather than sell off Columbia Grammar, as some on the board wanted to do, I was determined not only to "save" the school but to see it grow and prosper. But given our financial situation, the question was: How? Luckily, New York City at the time was trying to 'renew' the area in which the school was located. The West Side of Manhattan had seen a critical decline during and after World War II and had become one of New York's poorer neighborhoods. The school's trustees had at one point seriously considered moving the school to a new location but finally decided to remain at West 93rd Street when the city announced a program for renewal of the West Side.

In 1962, the city, state, and federal governments combined to create the West Side Urban Renewal project. Sixty-five sites were identified and numbered within a rectangle bordered by West 86th Street to the south, 96th Street to the north, Central Park West on the east, and Amsterdam Avenue on the west. These 65 sites were almost entirely comprised of empty parcels of land or substandard buildings, some of which were actually empty and boarded up. Other buildings were filled with squatters or low-income residents who had originally gotten their apartments through lawful means but were no longer paying rent. At the time, the area identified as the West Side Urban Renewal was one of the highest crime areas in New York. This is hard to imagine today when apartments are routinely going for more than a million dollars apiece and brownstones for more than $6 million, with the Upper West Side, particularly the West Side Urban Renewal areas, becoming one of the hottest, most gentrified areas in New York.

Nevertheless, in 1981, when I arrived at Columbia Grammar, it was far from clear whether the West Side Urban Renewal area was in a state of improvement or decline. The verdict was nowhere in sight, even though the project was already halfway through the planned 40-year urban renewal effort in which parcels of land were being put up for bid, generally 12 to 15 at a time, in what were called "amendments." I was there in time for public bids on the Fifth Amendment, or wave, of urban renewal projects. This Fifth Amendment had been open for bidding sometime in the mid-1970s but had yet to be resolved. The progress of the renewal program, as any large-scale government enterprise, was painfully slow.

Most of the projects proposed for the 13 sites of the Fifth Amendment involved either low income housing or high-end co-ops. The proponents for each of these two strata of the real estate market were seasoned fighters and very aggressively fought it out during meetings of Community Board 7. And into this political/social battlefield, Columbia Grammar and a few other intrepid not-for-profits gingerly entered the competition.

It seems that every community board in the city has a permanent cast of characters at any given time who are central to its operation. Community Board 7 reflected the Upper West Side and had more than its share of colorful, vocal, and ideological members who felt essentially that the future of New York City, meaning the fate of the city's poorest families, was riding on their shoulders. To my recollection, every one of those individuals, who represented the spirit and philosophy of Community Board 7, came out of the same basic mold: they were well educated, extremely liberal (to put it mildly), hard-working, usually in the arts or letters (newspapers, publishing, book stores, theaters, and so on), almost always of modest means themselves, and extremely aggressive. When around them, I had a sense that I was back in the early teens of the 20th century in Europe or the 1930s in America, leaning toward quasi communist party members (all of this said from a warm and positive slant), with the most laudable social goals being pursued with all their hearts and souls. Nothing was taken lightly, and certainly not the West Side Urban Renewal. Each site represented a battleground for all the social issues in the area of Community Board 7: rich against poor, Republican against Democrat, private real estate versus public access, and every other issue bearing down on New York then and even now as we look back on the grand fights in the 1970s and 1980s on the Upper West Side.

Columbia Grammar and Prep had formally submitted a proposal in the 1970s, indeed two separate proposals, for what were two parcels of land officially identified as Sites 23A and 23B, neither of which was either realistic or acceptable to Community Board 7, meaning to the local residents. Both sites, 23A and 23B, were located on West 93rd Street, diagonally across from our original building at 5 West 93rd, ideally situated for our school's dreamed-of expansion. Unfortunately, one of the sites, 23A, involved tearing down a parcel occupied by a low income building with no provision for the relocation or future residence of tenants in the building! In brief, I walked into a situation where the school was viewed as an "enemy of the people" and closely identified with the various rich developers who wanted to do similar things with other low-income housing on other West Side Urban Renewal sites. Many well-organized community advocacy groups (Stryckers Bay was one of many) existed primarily to block the efforts of developers and by extension of Columbia Grammar and Prep.

One of my first tasks was to re-think and re-develop our proposal through the West Side Urban Renewal bidding process. The fact that we had not a single dollar to our name, were $600,000-plus in the hole, with no prospects whatsoever to either raise money through a capital campaign or to borrow money through a bank or other type of mortgage lender, makes the story I am about to tell so compelling—and unlikely!

During my first month as headmaster, a gentleman dropped in on me who described himself as the head of the most successful and most active consulting firm for college and university capital expansion, fundraising, and planning in America. He said he had read an article about my appointment and just wanted to meet me. He certainly wasn't looking for business since anything Columbia Grammar and Prep might do would have been minuscule by his standards. In any event, he spent the good part of an afternoon with me, listening patiently to my plans and vision for the school. Ultimately, he gave me tremendous encouragement and, as it turned out, some very wise advice about how to proceed.

In a nutshell, this gentleman told me that I should be as bold as realistically possible regarding the future of the school with plans for two ambitious, comprehensive buildings for both sites, raise tuition to the level needed, plan a major fundraising campaign, and renew the board, bringing in new parents, especially those who would understandably have a large stake in the future of the school. He told me not to lose confidence and that nothing would get done of any worth except what was envisioned, pursued, and directed by a single voice, namely, the headmaster's.

To this day, I cannot recall his name and not that much of his appearance, other than that he was distinguished and successful looking, without specific features or details. It is one of those experiences that can be characterized as slightly mysterious but wonderfully encouraging because it bolstered my confidence at a time when I felt overwhelmed by the magnitude of Columbia Grammar and Prep's numerous problems. In fact, I rank this experience, whether it actually ever happened or not, as falling into the same category as finding Mike Mikrut, my indispensable maintenance head, by running across a pack of matches while pondering the very problem it solved! This timely visitor, while somewhat dream-like at this distant point in time, was nevertheless influential in a strangely positive way. In any respect, it was definitely one of the many examples of *kairos*, an event that happened at that perfect moment.

However, as you can appreciate, my situation required more than a dose of confidence to move forward with any degree of success at this point. First of all, I needed specific and realistic plans for new buildings on Sites 23A and 23B. With no time for elaborate planning, I basically worked with the school's architect (Pasanella and Klein) to develop plans for two buildings. But more importantly, I developed a proposal to reorganize Site 23A, the larger of the two parcels, to exclude the building occupied by low-income housing. Once armed with these plans for two new buildings, as well as a reconfigured Site 23A, I resubmitted our application to the City of New York, technically through the Department of Housing, Preservation and Development, and began one of the most colorful, draining, demoralizing, but ultimately exciting experiences of my life. In West Side Urban Renewal lingo, it was known as a ULURP procedure.

ULURP procedures were devised, I believe, by the devil to give sinners on this earth a taste of what might lie ahead in the afterworld. If you think ULURP, which stands for Urban Land Use Review Procedure, is a mouthful, you need to understand that it is actually a euphemism for what is in store for the initiate when he first enters this arcane world of urban redevelopment and planning.

While the two first steps of the ULURP procedure are relatively tame, it is with the third step, namely the community board, that all the fun begins. If you have never been to a community board meeting, you are missing one of the golden opportunities to experience grassroots democracy in America. New York City is divided up into 12 community board precincts. I had the added attraction of dealing with Community Board 7, which covered an area on the West Side full of community action groups of all stripes and colors, from those that seemed to be opposed to any and all progress to those who defined progress solely in terms of public housing and the needs of New York's ever-growing low-income families. While all these community groups had laudable goals, their *modus operandi,* was not always representative of the best elements of a democracy. To put it mildly, if you were on the "other side," then anything went as far as attacking you, and surprise!, I found that I was viewed as a member of the "other side." So began my trial by fire.

My first mistake, and therefore my first learning experience, was in bringing the school's lawyer and architect to the first community board meeting in October of 1981. It had never occurred to me that lawyers, and indeed architects who sat next to lawyers or represented anything other than low-income housing, were viewed as fascists/capitalists. And those sitting next to them, namely yours truly, were also placed in the same category. The associated mistake I made was having the lawyer and architect speak on behalf of the school. When it was clear that no one would ever be able to hear them over the shouts of "fascists, elitists," etc., we left with the agreement that we needed to take a different approach.

One could call it wisdom, but it was more necessity than anything else when I decided that, for better or for worse, I would attend the next community board meeting alone and did so for the next two and a half years. It took about six months of attending monthly meetings and sometimes semi-monthly meetings of subcommittees on planning and land use to overcome the initial hostility. I wore the same blue blazer, probably the same tie, but certainly the same gray pants to every meeting for two and a half years, finally getting across the point that we were a poor school, not a rich school; that we were representative of the population at large, not exclusive; that we were out to renew the neighborhood with a needed mission—schooling—for a wide range of kids; that we were going to be part of what would make a healthy urban environment even healthier; that we would maintain our long-standing efforts to have a minimum of 20 percent minority families in the school (though it came at great expense to the other families because we had no endowment funds); and that our outreach to the community would remain strong with one of the most successful, long-standing, and active community service requirements of any private school in the city. In brief, we were indeed a worthy candidate for community support.

It was not only a sensible argument but a sensible and positive prospect for the Upper West Side. Doris Rosenblum, one of the shortest, most feisty, and warmest of all characters on Community Board 7, recognized this, bless her soul, and insisted in her very forceful manner that others listen respectfully and consider in a fair way the merits of my position. Doris was irrepressible and totally fearless. After she watched my getting bashed repeatedly by her fellow members at the community board meetings in my early months as headmaster, she decided to take me under her considerable wings. And for that, I thank my lucky stars, and the entire school community should as well! From then on, it seemed as if I had General Patton guarding my left flank and the Mafia guarding my right. Thus, I started experiencing my first thaw in the cold war that I had walked into at Community Board 7.

When I look back, I try to understand what might have appealed to Doris at the time. It must have been my status as underdog, coming as I did to the meetings alone, and the fact that I had shown enough mettle to take her colleagues' best shots without flinching. And then too, I came back for more. At some point, she accepted my view that this little private school—along with the Claremont Riding Stables and Ballet Hispanico, the other two not-for-profits contending for sites in this Fifth Amendment to the West Side Urban Renewal—would indeed fit right into a sanely balanced renewal program for this part of New York City. After all, I argued repeatedly, if diversity was to have an honest meaning for the Upper West Side, it included low-income and middle-income housing, private schools as well as public schools, private riding stables as well as public parks, and so on. Columbia Grammar and Prep had been a very important part of the Upper West Side since 1907, had been a good neighbor to all, and deserved an opportunity to expand its facilities, without which it faced almost certain demise.

And so with a sound argument and the invaluable assistance of Doris Rosenblum, we went from an initial vote in 1981 in which less than 10 percent approved our bid for Sites 23A and 23B to two and a half years later when the 50 voting members of the community board voted 49 to 0 (with one abstention) in our favor. We went from pariah to a welcome addition to the expanded group of renewal projects on the Upper West Side. To this day, I am proud to say that with few exceptions, the community remains entirely supportive of our growth and renewal. After all, Community Board #7 has gone on to approve seven additional building projects for our school over the following 28 years—proof in the pudding!

At one point, when it was clear we would win the bidding process for Sites 23A and 23B, a serious problem arose that threatened to put an end to our prospects for acquiring the land. The city stipulated, and essentially refused to budge, that whoever became the successful bidder for Sites 23A and 23B would not only have to break ground but begin building within 90 days on *both* parcels of land. How were we, with no money at all, to build on Site 23A, the larger of the two sites at approximately 12,500 square feet, and on Site 23B which was 8,000 square feet, at the same time? In 1982 dollars, even modest buildings on each site would have cost about $10 million, a totally unattainable sum of money for the school in those days.

By December of my second year, I was ready to throw in the towel and abandon any prospect of getting Sites 23A and 23B because of the city's inflexible requirements. But a few days before Christmas in 1982, I got together with Doris and four or five of her lady friends who were also members of Community Board 7 with some last-ditch ideas I had developed. One idea was to build only on the front half of Site 23A, which represented 7,500 square feet with a 75-foot front, and to create a simple play yard on the rear until we could add on to the building at a later point. The other idea, which was even more fanciful, was to ask for a five-year extension on Site 23B. I thought the only possible way I could get the city to consider these ideas seriously was to have Doris visit the city's attorney at Housing, Preservation and Development with me, which she did. We sat down with the city's top land-use lawyer who heard me out. She seemed to think it was an interesting idea, though one that had never been proposed before as far as she knew. Eventually, I drew up some language that incorporated both provisions in a proposal, which she said the city would consider in formal terms based on approval by the full community board.

The next community board meeting took place in February. When I entered the large public space of a low income housing project near Lincoln Center, I saw the room packed with community people. In fact, it was the most substantial crowd I had ever seen at a community board meeting, with numerous people with placards denouncing rich developers, elitists, etc., with all sorts of slogans that suggested a hostile environment and an unsuccessful meeting for Columbia Grammar. It turned out all the hubbub was over some other project somewhere on the West Side that had engendered extreme anger within Community Board 7; it had absolutely nothing to do with the school. To make a wild evening short, I presented my proposal to the angriest and largest crowd I had ever faced, with no one seeming to listen or hear anything I said. The result was that my proposal passed for no other reason than to get me out of the way to move on to discussion of the other contentious project.

Armed with this unanimous approval, I went back to Housing, Preservation and Development with the truthful report that Community Board 7 had signed off with no objections, and we ultimately got the five-year extension approved by the Board of Estimate. Such are the vagaries of life—timing is the essence—or once again, a welcome instance of *Kairos*.

CHEMICAL BANK AND NAN MILLER: ANOTHER GUARDIAN ANGEL

And so is money. How were we going to pay for any of this? The school was insolvent in the fall of 1981 and only barely less insolvent two years later when we were supposed to actually build a new building. Just how we ended up paying for our new building was another instance of serendipity at work.

From day one, the issue of financing the buildings was discussed at my community board meetings and meetings with Housing, Preservation and Development. And from the beginning my position was that the school would initiate a capital campaign led by the new headmaster that would generate the funds to construct these new buildings. However, there was one troubling bit of history. I soon learned from the school's records, honest confessions from trustees who had been around, and parents who had been at the school for a few years, not to mention alumni who considered it a standing joke, that the school had had a series of failed capital campaigns over the course of two decades. Some of the campaigns were non-starters, others were aborted early on, and a few were carried out more or less to the finish but without raising any more money than was gobbled up by various architects and ending up with pie-in-the-sky plans for buildings that never got built on land that was never acquired. In brief, the school's track record was abysmal, to put it mildly, and the city had gotten wind of the many unsuccessful past attempts. Consequently, the city insisted that I prove to their satisfaction that I could be successful where others had failed.

What we agreed upon, the school and the city, was that a feasibility study would be carried out by a reputable firm to determine or assess the prospects for a capital campaign. This was carried out in the fall of 1982, during my second year, with the bottom line result that we could possibly raise $3.2 million but were more likely to raise something around $2 million—at best. It was for this reason, among others, that I came up with the concept of building simply on the front of 23A with a play yard on the back and a five-year postponement of building on Site 23B. The architects indicated that roughly $3 million to $3.5 million was sufficient to build a four-story building on the front side of 23A. Since we had no money at that point for any capital project, $3.5 million could just as soon be $35 million.

What to do? It was time for a walk. After all, I had found the pack of matches and consequently Mike Mikrut on a walk–but a mortgage?

And so sometime during that fall of my second year, I was walking down Sixth Avenue when I noticed a bronze plaque on the wall of a building that read "Chemical Bank, Not-For-Profit." "Not-For-Profit," I thought to myself, "now that sounds interesting. We are a not-for-profit school. I wonder what that's all about?"

I went into the building and was directed to the second floor where there was a receptionist. After a few telephone calls, a young lady escorted me to one of the multitude of cubicles, where I met another one of the angels in this story, Nan Miller. Nan was one of the many "Assistant Vice Presidents for Whatever" at Chemical Bank, which has long since merged with Manufacturers Hanover and ultimately Chase and J.P. Morgan. In any event, this very nice woman heard my story about a small Upper West Side private school, its long-standing attempt to acquire land, and its need to have some kind of immediate funding or proof of such in order to be accepted as a bidder for a site through the Urban Renewal program.

Nan seemed to love the story and loved the situation. Far from discouraging me, she encouraged me to come up with a 10-year financial profile based on the buildings that would ultimately grace Sites 23A and 23B as proof to her, and more importantly to her bosses, that Columbia Grammar could manage to pay back this loan when so many other private schools in recent years had not. At least two private schools on the West Side alone could not pay back the money they had borrowed from banks at the time, but the banks didn't want to be in the awkward position of defaulting on mortgages and seizing property since that meant closing the schools and dealing with enormous parental wrath and bad public relations.

I therefore had to make an extremely strong case, and that was no easy task. I was creating a 10-year budget projection based on buildings that weren't there, enrollment that was purely imaginary, heat and electrical costs that could only be vaguely determined, and space dimensions that changed with the constantly evolving plans and layout of the science labs, gym, library, etc. Nevertheless, I came up with an exquisitely detailed 10-year projection on a yellow legal pad which, thanks to the treasurer of the board's fancy computers, was translated into a Lotus spreadsheet that all in all looked quite impressive.

After a year of various manipulations and "scientific" adjustments, the bank, through the goodness of Nan Miller's heart and her untiring advocacy of the school's future, awarded us a $3.5 million construction loan through the Chemical Bank Not-For-Profit division. By the way, I discovered early on that "Not-For-Profit" did not refer to the fact that the bank was not making any profit; it referred to the fact that it was making a good deal of profit from a not-for-profit! Profit or not, the fact remains that if it were not for the warm heart and broad mind of Nan Miller, Columbia Grammar and Prep School, not to mention this headmaster, would not be talking about our three decades of growth and renewal!

THE PANAM, SEARS, AND COLUMBIA GRAMMAR BUILDINGS: TITANS TO THE RESCUE

Building in New York City is an adventure. Various groups manage to find a way to get involved in any building project in the city. Some are called unions, others are called coalitions, and others are called contractors, subcontractors, and trades. Whatever the name, they are far more experienced in the process of building a building than the unsuspecting and overoptimistic, always naive "owner." Architects make these pretty designs, lovely facades, and seemingly perfect interiors, giving you the sense that this new project is just around the corner, if only you would sign on the dotted line. But once you embark on a new project, the real life experience of dealing with all these characters begins, and reality soon sets in. Doing a minor kitchen repair is difficult enough; putting up a new building with 50 to 60 subcontractors is altogether a different experience. Here's what the school faced when, in the fall of 1984, we wanted to break ground for our long-awaited new high school building.

The city, the state, the federal government, and the community board, through the West Side Urban Renewal, had approved our project with a number of stipulations. The most serious was the requirement that we build within the $3.5 million limit, which represented the outer limit of our fundraising potential, as determined by the feasibility study. The architects, therefore, designed a four-story building that covered only half the site to keep within the $3.5 million budget. The first problem we faced was that the projected cost of the new building, even though it had been reduced in scope and size, still came to $3.5 to $4 million based on a professional estimator's analysis. The next problem was that the bidding process, seeking a contractor, produced bids in the $4.5 to $5 million range with none lower. While Chemical Bank was willing to go up to $3.5 million on its construction loan, the city was insisting that we find a contractor who would build this building within the $3.5 million limit. What to do?

At that time, David Steinmann, a parent in the school whose older daughter had just entered the previous year and whose two younger sons would follow her soon thereafter, had told me that a famous builder named Carl Morse attended their synagogue and asked me if I wanted him to approach Morse. He might be able to suggest a builder for us, or in some way help us deal with this difficult, seemingly insurmountable problem of finding a builder at a much lower cost. Carl Morse, if you didn't know, was the principal of Morse Diesel, the builder responsible for some of the finest buildings in America, including the Sears Tower in Chicago, the tallest building in America; the PanAm Building in New York; and many other extraordinary skyscrapers built in New York and around the world.

Morse, who was retired at that time and in his early 80s, volunteered to meet with me and give us some free advice. Not only was Carl Morse's advice most welcome, but it also turned out to be one of the most productive, helpful, and colorful relationships in my life. Despite his age, Morse was totally undiminished in terms of quickness of mind, strength of body, determination, willpower, and just plain feistiness. He quickly agreed to take on the project *pro bono* as the construction manager and overseer of this worthy effort to give Columbia Grammar and Prep a new and expanded home.

Morse's first decision was that our proposed steel frame building should instead be built using post-tension concrete. This was a relatively new and untried way of supporting a building at the time, and in fact our high-school building became only the second building in New York City to use it. Post-tension concrete involves pouring high density concrete around steel rods that are slowly stretched while the concrete hardens, creating, as the name indicates, a high degree of tension at each of the two posts. We have a full-sized gym ceiling that is held up by six of these beams stretched 75 feet from end to end at enormous tension. Although the thought of this scared me at first, numerous architects, including our own, along with Carl Morse himself, assured me over and over that this process was safe, sound, and long lasting. (It certainly has proved to be the case for the first two decades. I screen various points of the building for any cracks, even hairline cracks, but have yet to spot the first one.) The big plus for us was that post-tension concrete was a much cheaper process than steel. In 1984, for reasons that had to do with complex market conditions, making a steel-framed building was prohibitively expensive on our limited budget.

This was one of the key steps of controlling costs, but there were hundreds of others, both large and small, that Carl Morse's leadership and unique status in the building world allowed us to make. For example, Carl found our bricks from "extras" on other big projects that had over-ordered, as well as an elevator that had been ordered for another project that turned out to be surplus, and an excavator who gave us a special deal just because of Carl. For the west foundation of the building, Carl talked the structural engineer into using stacked rock, as was the norm back at the turn of the century, instead of a much more expensive foundation. And so on.

Carl would meet me on the construction site at about 7:00 every morning, and we would walk through the project together, whether it was at the excavating stage or the building stage. He would berate workers, change plans on the spot, talk about techniques that were too newfangled and fancy for him, and basically make a complete nuisance of himself while making it clear to everyone that he was in charge of every detail, large and small, and that this building, in spite of the usual building schedules, was going to be built from start to finish in 12 months.

That was a nearly impossible goal, given that in August of 1984, we still did not own the property. While the city had approved our bid through the West Side Urban Renewal, we had yet to close on the property, which involved complex contracts through Housing, Preservation and Development, Urban Planning, and ultimately approval by the Board of Estimate, an archaic commission comprised of the five borough presidents and other appointees. (The Board of Estimate no longer exists.) In brief, by the time September 1st rolled around, we were, at best, still about a month away from closing on the property. Both sites were still enclosed by 10- or 12-foot chain-link fences with thick locks on the heavy gates facing 93rd Street. And we all knew that if we didn't begin by September 1, there would be absolutely no chance of the building being ready the following September.

While I was pondering the dilemma of losing this critical month of

September to get started on our project, I heard one of the loudest rumblings I had ever heard. Our building began trembling and vibrating. Surely this had to be an earthquake, I thought.

But this incredible noise turned out to be the biggest bulldozer I had ever seen in my life. It was thundering down 93rd Street from Central Park West, carving four inch ruts into the street. I ran up to the bulldozer and asked the operator what he was doing.

"Morse Diesel sent me to start clearing this site," replied the husky driver.

"Wait a minute," I said, "we don't own the site yet, please hold on a second," and I ran into my office and called our lawyer, who said, "Don't let him get on the site. We don't own the property and the city will crucify us if we enter the site before we own the land."

I called Carl Morse next and told him that the lawyer just said not to proceed until we actually owned the land. I will never forget what he said: "All lawyers are horses' asses. You want that building next year, we're going into the property now."

With some type of walkie-talkie setup they used to communicate with the truck that had brought the bulldozer to the site, Carl insisted in the way that only Carl could insist, that work proceed *immediately*. The bulldozer then ran up on the sidewalk, crushed the concrete, broke down the fence, and commenced work.

This was Carl Morse, someone I grew to love and appreciate over the next 12 months, who could bulldoze every problem large and small. Whether it was a trade union dispute or a structural engineering issue stemming from the architectural design (Carl ranked architects along with lawyers), there was never anyone who could say, "This can't be done that way," or "That is not in the plans," or "We don't have the money for air conditioning." Every problem got solved and got solved quickly with Carl in charge. Carl took on the project with heart and soul, and much to everyone's disbelief and surprise—architects, builders, subcontractors, neighbors, the city of New York, and Chemical Bank—our building was built in 12 months. The school started on time with the largest enrollment in Columbia Grammar and Prep's history.

Who was this Carl Morse? Carl Morse did not have an imposing physique, but he was what you call a diamond in the rough. Most of the time, like a sailor on leave with a few drinks under his belt, his language was colorful and he was always ready for a fight or a risqué joke. At the same time, he was cultured, intelligent, well educated, and deeply wise. He just didn't have as much fun with that side of his personality and life as he did with the Jake LaMotta side. He enjoyed rough language and fighting and conflict but always within reason and always for a purpose. Thankfully, during 1984-1985, it was for the extraordinary purpose of giving us a wonderful new building.

Problems never intimidated Carl. He would resolve them with the wave of his powerful hand and pick up the pieces later. He literally could grab a phone and talk to anyone, whether it was a commissioner, mayor, or some high-powered lawyer. Everybody who was anyone in the city government knew Carl and respected him. As the year unfolded, it turned out that Carl needed every bit of his communication skills and strength of character to get through some of the challenges we found ourselves in at various times.

For example, while we were working on the fourth and "final" floor of our new high school building, which was two floors above our gym, I mentioned to Carl one day that it would be great to have an additional floor, a fifth floor devoted solely to science. When Carl heard that comment, which I had said rather wistfully and off the top of my head, he said, "Let's build it." The fact that we had no plans for a fifth floor and had nearly completed the fourth with the roof ready to go on were simply minor obstacles to Carl. He quickly called the architect and told him to design a fifth floor, and he wanted the plans by Monday, a few days after. If you know anything about the planning process in New York City, we would, of course, have to submit plans to the building department, planning department, get those approved and double checked for safety conditions, etc., all before we received a permit to build. To build another floor on a building without having gone through this lengthy process was unheard of—and strictly against the law.

In fact, shortly before, a similar incident had occurred in New York on the East Side where a developer had added four stories or so to a high rise apartment building without approval. Since each story was a duplicate of the one below, he already had the plans, but the fact remained that the city hadn't approved these additional stories. Well, the developer was forced to remove the four stories brick by brick at tremendous cost. That incident supposedly sent a loud and clear message to all New Yorkers: Pay strict attention to the proper procedures involved in getting a building approved in New York City.

But Carl Morse was not one to take this kind of warning too seriously. His reaction was to say, "If you need another floor, let's build it." Not only did we not have approval, architectural plans, or any other required preparation for this additional floor, we didn't have the money, given the fact that our $3.5 million construction loan didn't actually cover the cost of the four-story building, much less a five-story building. None of these "little details" made much of an impact on Carl. If the school was going to be better with five stories rather than four, then we would build it—and after all, America needed more science labs.

As you might expect, the architect didn't have the plan for the fifth floor ready on Monday as Carl had asked. But Carl ordered his workers to start adding a fifth floor anyway. A few weeks later, the architect finally finished his work, and though I am fuzzy on the chronology, four to six weeks later, when the bricks had gone up and the flooring was already put in, the plans for the fifth floor were submitted to the city. The city, however, had already gotten wind of what we were up to, and the commissioner of buildings called Carl Morse and me and about 50 subcontractors down to the building department for an emergency meeting.

The 50 of us sat on one one side and the commissioner sat on the other in one of the largest conference rooms I have ever seen. The commissioner then spent a half hour reading us the riot act, saying he could put all of us in jail, not just Carl and the headmaster but every single subcontractor as well. He had already made one builder remove some unauthorized floors, and he would not let us have one illegally. For the first and only time, I heard Carl Morse apologize. Very thoughtfully, nicely, and meekly, by Carl's standards anyway, he explained the situation and talked about the improvement to the building and the needs of the school and asked for forgiveness on our behalf for what ultimately was his initiative and decision. I followed with a quietly specific rundown of the school's needs, its population, its long history of struggles on the Upper West Side, and its chance finally to become a reputable school once again with a well-rounded academic program in which science would be strengthened among other important improvements. After two hours of give and take, the commissioner said he would let us know our fate the next day.

Much to my surprise, we didn't end up in jail. On the contrary, we were given approval to proceed, although with the strongest possible reprimand, but with no requirement to retrace our steps and settle for less. And thus, the science center at Columbia Grammar and Prep was born. (The reader might find it interesting to note that we have had four Intel science competition semi-finalists over the past decade, the largest number from a single private school in New York City, possibly of any private school in New York State.)

One critical stumbling block remained: We still had to approach Chemical Bank regarding the new level of expenses created by this addition. But once again, after a number of meetings where I quietly described the needs of the school, the importance of the science floor, the fact that the building would now be complete and balanced academically, the bank decided to increase the construction loan from $3.5 to $5.2 million.

The last major hurdle was complete except for actually getting the building physically open for the first day of school, a chaotic but quite exciting and vibrant beginning to the 1985-86 school year. Our plan was to open the building on two floors, the third and fourth, with the science floor opening a month later, the gym yet another month later, and the basement last of all. School took place over the course of the first two and a half months with fire marshals posted on every floor, as well as areas prohibited to students and faculty which were for workers only. It all gave the school an energetic, hard-hat feel, but a lovely one with a sense of significant progress taking place. This whole complicated, layered opening arrangement was something that Carl navigated through the city bureaucracy, allowing us to proceed in this unique step-by-step fashion. By December 1st, everything had finally been completed, and we ended up with a beautiful and functional high-school building that gave us the ideal environment for a college preparatory program. Without Carl Morse, it could never have been accomplished. He was truly our guardian angel.

One last anecdote regarding Carl. When we opened the first floor of the new building, I invited our first graders over to see the new building and to meet Carl Morse. As kindergartners the year before, during the construction, they had been following the progress by making little drawings of the building going up floor by floor while they stood across the street. I thought it would be fun and appropriate if I had them all come over to the new building, give them each an Eskimo Pie, and meet Mr. Morse, who had built our building.

So Carl was next to me while the first graders were seated on the floor of the soon to be high-school library eating their ice cream, when I introduced Mr. Morse as the man who not only built our building, but someone who had built many great buildings, including the tallest building in America. One of the little kids said, "Oh, you mean the Empire State Building," but another quickly corrected him, "No, you mean, the Sears building in Chicago!" Carl thought that was one of the most wonderful moments of his life, as he put it. He said the young kids today—his own children were all grown up—were so bright and their futures so full of promise that building Columbia Prep's high school had meant more to him than the Sears building. It was the fulfillment of his career as a builder.

A builder who had a special knack for balancing budgets, I might add. Although we owed $785,000 in change orders or overruns on the building, we ended up paying zero. Several goons sent by the subcontractors on more than one occasion had come to my office to threaten me unless we paid up—mentioning the fact that there was plenty of leftover concrete for other purposes, and so on. But when Carl heard about it, he put an end to it. Frankly, I think they would have happily carried out their less-than-veiled threats had it not been for Carl's timely intervention. As Carl was wont to say, building a new building in New York is not for sissies.

PETER KALIKOW: AN ALTOGETHER NEW LEVEL OF SUCCESS!

One might naturally assume that with a new 40,000 square-foot high school building finally at hand after a 30-year wait, Columbia Grammar would now feel secure about its future. But we still lacked such essentials as an adequate and full-sized cafeteria, an honest-to-goodness theater (rather than converting the gym three times a year into a makeshift substitute), studios for art and music, and offices for a much-expanded cadre of learning specialists to help our students succeed in a demanding college preparatory program. We had a lot of land for all this—as we still had the back half of Site 23A to complete and all of Site 23B—but no money at all to build even one more, not to mention two more buildings. And given the hard-pressed times of the mid-1980s and our still less-than-developed fundraising capacity, the prospect of finding the funding for a major capital expansion seemed far off into the future. The reality was that we were still "broke" financially—and we also had a $5.2 million dollar mortgage that had to be re-paid—relentlessly—on a monthly basis. We needed a lot of help if we were to ever meet even a small portion of the many lofty goals still before us. In brief, we needed another "guardian angel." That person would end up being Mary Kalikow's husband, Peter.

Peter Kalikow, as most any New Yorker is aware, has been one of the most successful builder/developers in a city filled with such titans and, fortunately for us, a parent at the school. When he turned his undivided attention to helping us accomplish our many goals, there was no question of "whether," but simply "how soon." After helping us successfully apply for tax-exempt bonds through the Industrial Development Agency, which gave us long-term and low-interest funding for a new building, Peter, with his entire staff of construction managers, engineers, and architects, served as our "construction manager" supreme, all *pro bono* and even more important, with a personal "guarantee" that the new building would be built in a year and on budget. And that's what happened.

As you might recall, I had asked the City early on for a five-year extension for building on our second West Side Urban Renewal Site #23B. However, given our continuing financial pressures, even with our new high school building, the five-year extension was generously extended another five years, giving us enough time to strengthen our financial base as well as solidify our growing enrollment. Consequently, when Peter Kalikow offered to be our new "Carl Morse," we were ready to accept his extraordinary offer, and within one brief whirlwind of a year, we had yet another 42,500 square-foot building with a spacious new cafeteria/kitchen, our first "real" theater (as previously mentioned, plays and concerts were always held in a makeshift fashion in one of our two gyms), art and music studios, more science labs and classrooms, LRC offices, and a beautiful new office for the headmaster that I have enjoyed and appreciated every day since this gorgeous building opened in the mid-1990s.

And as if that weren't enough for any school to enjoy for the good part of a century, Peter followed up this building with an equally spectacular addition to the high school, a 30,000 square-foot facility that contained an even larger and more professional theater, providing additional science labs and classrooms, and yet another full-sized gym—once again, all built from beginning to end within a year and on budget. This last new building project gave us arguably the finest physical plant among private schools, at least in Manhattan, where such essentials as gyms, theaters, cafeterias, and libraries are often undersized or absent altogether. This once small, bankrupt school of 36,000 square feet of run-down space with one small gym, now boasted over 150,000 square feet, most of it new and state of the art, with seven science labs, three gyms, three libraries, four computer labs, three cafeterias, two theatres, an abundance of classrooms and nearly 20 offices for reading, math, and LRC specialists—along with our original 1924 swimming pool, fully renovated! We had indeed come a long way, but the story was far from complete. We subsequently added four additional brownstones to our lower school and yet another gym (a total of four), with a fifth brownstone in the wings, as I write (a total of nine in a row).

However, our three new buildings, built as part of the West Side Urban

Renewal, constitute without question the transitional years when we went from bankruptcy to being one of the finest, most reputable and successful—not to mention, most sought-after schools in the city. Without having two veritable titans of development working tirelessly and *pro bono* on our behalf—Peter Kalikow and Carl Morse—we could never have accomplished what appeared to virtually any observer as risky and foolhardy, if not downright impossible. Our status as a "second tier" New York private school would prove to be short-lived. We were now well on our way to regaining the "top tier" status that Columbia Grammar had enjoyed for nearly two centuries.

PART 2:

ANNUAL FUNDS AND ALL THINGS FINANCIAL

*"We can't solve problems by using the same kind of thinking
we used when we created them."*
—Albert Einstein

INTRODUCTION

The thesis of this section of the book, "All Things Financial," can be reduced to a simple and oft-repeated dictum: *Live within your means,* or in the case of private schools: *Operate your school on tuition alone.* Indeed, learning how, as Columbia Grammar has through the years, to live on tuition alone constitutes the core of our management philosophy as well as our success and renewal as a school. In those early days, living on tuition alone was admittedly our only option. We had no other choice. However, long after we had other choices—for example, to supplement our operating budget through annual funds and the like—we chose, consciously and deliberately, to stick with this simple and straightforward approach. We did not do this out of Stoicism or a stubborn sense of pride. Rather, it seemed intuitively clear to me at least, even at that early stage of my tenure, that an ever-increasing dependence on voluntary gifts, though obviously helpful in the short run—a quick fix, so to speak—would get us nowhere, at least nowhere particularly desirable, in the long run. But even I, in my most exaggerated dreams for the school, could not have envisioned at that early stage the true scope of the many and varied benefits that would result from following this somewhat old-fashioned, but time-tested principle: *Live within your means.*

Relying solely on tuition to operate our school freed up, over the span of three decades, millions of dollars for growth and renewal, resulting in a complete transformation of the school, taking us, as it has, from the bottom to the very top tier of private education in New York City. Here are only some of the more prominent features of this transformation:

• We went from 36,000 square feet of sub-standard and deteriorating space to nearly 200,000, maintained on a daily basis at the highest levels of safety and care.

• We built three modern buildings in one of the most challenging and expensive environments known to man, in the heart of New York City.

• We added four fully renovated brownstones to our campus, with a fifth in the works as I write, giving us nine in a row, in the Historic District of the Upper West Side, today one of the most desirable and sought after real estate areas in Manhattan—not to mention, most expensive.

- Living on tuition alone, moreover, has been the single most important reason we have been able to raise teacher salaries from the bottom to the top tier in New York City. Starting in the fall of 2012, for example, just a few months from now, *a beginning teacher with no experience* will start at $70,000 with full benefits, the highest starting salary in the city, public or private. (Just three short years ago, we were the first and only school to pay a beginning teacher with no experience $60,000, and we are determined to be the first in a few more years to start a beginning teacher at $80,000.)

- Along the way, we were able to double the school's contribution to the individual retirement accounts of our teachers and staff from 4 percent to 8, and to pay 100 percent of an individual teacher's medical premiums, and keep it that way through these difficult economic times, when many private schools have been forced to cut back on benefits, medical and otherwise.

- And perhaps best of all, we have been able to provide more and more financial aid over the years—without an endowment—to an ever more diverse student body, surpassing $5 million in aid for the present school year, 2011-2012—*all paid for out of tuition income*!

- And finally, to answer your obvious suspicion: No, the school is not deeply in debt as you might understandably assume, given our high salaries and benefits, not to mention new buildings and five new brownstones. The rest of the world, from Greece and Ireland to back home in the United States, might be over-leveraged and swimming in debt so deep that it might never be repaid, but our school now has a physical plant valued at well over $200 million with *no debt* whatsoever. It's true: We have gone from insolvency to owners of one of the finest physical plants of any private school in perhaps the priciest real estate market in America during three decades of non-stop growth and renewal—*without a dollar of outstanding debt.*

- And you might also be thinking that since going into debt is not the answer to all these new buildings and expansion, then surely it must be tuition income itself—in other words, we must be charging more than others, or how else can we account for all this non-stop growth and renewal over the years? Well, that's not the answer either, since we can—and later will—show that our tuition and fee levels have remained at the mid-point or lower among the 16 most competitive private K-12 schools in New York City for over 25 years of keeping detailed records.

• And very lastly, one of the most important and far-ranging benefits of all has to do with the environment or atmosphere of the school: learning to live within our means forced us to *streamline our administrative structure and keep it that way*. While more difficult to quantify than new buildings and similar physical improvements, keeping our administrative hierarchy, especially middle management (for want of a better term), at the bare minimum has allowed us to concentrate all our energy and time, in addition to money, on the needs of students and faculty—and not on *administrative bloat and wastefulness* or to mention the single greatest cause of waste in any institution: *administrators making work for other administrators*! While harder to put a price tag on and more often than not hidden from public view in any bureaucracy, a streamlined management has been one of the keys to our success—and, as you will shortly see—the main reason why other private schools run (and must run, given the way they are managed) ever larger operating deficits just to break even each year.

This book, therefore, and especially this section, "All Things Financial," represents an opportunity for us to share our philosophy and experience with others, particularly heads of school, trustees, parents, and all those concerned with the long-term health and well-being of their schools. That being said, my strong suspicion is that not many of my fellow school heads, except perhaps those starting out new to such a career, are going to appreciate what I have to say about how best to run a private school. The main reason for my pessimism has to do with the fact that I am admittedly highly critical in the following pages of some of the most commonplace and long-standing practices of virtually all private schools, but especially the universal practice of supplementing an operating budget with ever greater voluntary giving, what is innocently and universally called by all private schools the *annual fund*. After all, no one can be expected to enjoy, much less welcome, being told that what they have been doing and continue to do in their schools for as far back as anyone can remember is fundamentally flawed and ought to be re-examined from top to bottom. However, even though it might not be welcome advice, the fact is that the practice of relying on voluntary gifts for much of a school's operating expenses is both wrongheaded and ultimately self-defeating and in my view diverts attention and energy away from the pursuit of more important long-term goals, the very goals we have been able as a school to achieve over these past three decades.

Moreover, the sheer amounts raised each year, numbering as they do in the millions at many of our most illustrious and best known schools, have become embarrassingly—and dangerously—large. While annual funds clearly serve the immediate purpose of balancing a school's budget, they are nevertheless pernicious to the long-term health and well-being of any private school, as we will see in very great detail in the following pages.

In this regard, what has particularly puzzled and indeed frustrated me over the years, however, is that the pros and cons of fundraising are *never* questioned, not even discussed in professional circles by heads of school. It is universally assumed and basically taken for granted that "annual giving," even on ever larger and larger scales, constitutes an unqualified virtue. The fact is, however, private school assumptions about fundraising, no matter how strongly and universally held, are far from unqualified truths—and their merits and demerits ought to be discussed and debated *in the open* by heads of school, trustees, faculty, and parents alike. And the only way to start this long overdue discussion is to recognize that there are in fact some very serious and troubling problems that need to be addressed. "All Things Financial" is my attempt to bring these issues to the light of day, so that private school communities can begin to address these problems in a constructive fashion.

While I generally refrain from going to academic association meetings, particularly the annual meeting of the National Association of Independent Schools and the New York State Association of Independent Schools as well, I do make an effort to review their published programs and agendas on a regular basis to see what topics are being addressed. Never once in my three decades have I ever seen the topic of "deficit spending" or the universal use of annual funds to "close the gaps" in the operating budgets of private schools listed on an agenda—not even a modest workshop or group discussion, much less as the overall focus of an annual gathering of school heads as the topic deserves. Yes, there is much talk about "financial sustainability" these days and related topics having to do with school finances and budgets. However, all these discussions and themes, as far as I can determine, are premised on maintaining the status quo—never questioning it. The advice that comes out of these national and statewide gatherings of administrators invariably boils down to doing more, not less, of what schools have always done to solve financial problems, namely, to raise more and more money through annual giving to "close a school's ever-larger operating deficit," and to raise more in endowment funds at the same time to further supplement a school's daily needs. The fact is, however, that the very opposite is true—and we have three decades of evidence to back up that claim, as I will explain in some detail in the following pages.

It will not surprise me at all, therefore, to find that my little book has received a frosty reception from school associations and school leaders alike when it finally rolls off the presses. Change is rarely welcome in academic circles, and old habits die slowly and reluctantly, if at all. My strong guess is that both groups—school heads and association leaders—will particularly disapprove of the fact that I have brought these issues to the public's attention in the first place, especially in this seemingly harsh and uncompromising fashion—an instance of washing dirty linen in public, if you will. Messengers bringing bad news have rarely experienced a warm reception, and I certainly don't expect to be an exception to this ancient rule. All I can say at this point, however, is that the "bad" news is only temporary. If you, as a school head, are willing to make the necessary changes in how you operate your school, if you indeed actually carry out some of these changes as the opportunities arise, I promise you that our message will ultimately serve as good—and not bad—news for your school.

I cannot refrain from telling you a brief story at this point dating from some years back. It is perhaps the simplest way to illustrate for readers outside the professional school establishment the surprising and almost total antipathy that exists towards any serious challenge to conventional thinking or "business as usual" on the part of those who should in fact be the most interested parties in the first place. The long-standing director (to go unnamed) of one of the most respected professional organizations (also to go unnamed) regularly visited me at my school, at least once a year, simply to have lunch and chat, over a period of 15 years or so. His reason for doing so, he would say, had to do with the fact that I never came to the annual conference of the association he headed (in fact, the last such conference I attended was 27 years ago!)—hence his annual visits to see me for lunch and keep in touch. He also admitted that he greatly enjoyed capital projects, and I always, to his great pleasure and curiosity, seemed to be engaged in one building project or another. He was particularly curious as to how I financed so many projects, one after the other, with no capital campaigns, feasibility studies, or endless committee meetings! *What was the secret?* During the course of our many discussions over lunch, my good director friend would invariably try to talk me into coming to the next annual conference, especially since—at least according to him—I would more often than not quite literally be the only school head from that association not attending. I was passing up, after all, all this collegiality, stimulating conversation and networking, not to mention all this wonderful food and drink. For my part, I always made him the very same offer in return: I will happily come to the next annual conference, if he will put me on the agenda to talk about the risks and pitfalls of *deficit spending*, i.e. the ever increasing reliance on voluntary gifts—annual funds and endowment income—to balance a school's operating budget. I explained to him on more than one occasion the "secret" of our success, in simple but clear terms, how our willingness to live on tuition alone all these many years and to never use a dollar of voluntary giving to operate our school were the primary keys to our success. It needn't remain a secret, I assured him: I was more than happy to share our experience with all my colleagues. It was this simple and straightforward approach to managing a school that answered his ongoing questions as to how all this growth and renewal happened over the years, and I was perfectly happy to see it adopted by all the other schools in his association.

However, my director/colleague never once took me up on my offer, and on one of his last visits—before he retired—he admitted what I had always understood or at least guessed to be at the core of his reluctance to have the issue aired in the open. He said, and this is a literal quote, *"If I let you talk about all that, they will string me up on the nearest oak tree!"* Remember Giuseppe! Certain things are simply viewed by private school heads as so central to their success, even survival, that contemplating life without them is apparently more than they can bear. Receiving an annual infusion of ever larger voluntary funds to close the inevitable and ever larger "gap" in a school's operating budget is just one of those core beliefs—and my director/colleague and I both knew quite well that raising the issue was not going to be welcomed by my fellow school heads. By the way, I subsequently made the same offer to his temporary replacement when the search for his successor was underway, even more recently, with the same awkward but polite refusal. It should go without saying that I am still hopeful of receiving an invitation to talk about my favorite subject at a future gathering of my colleagues at one of their annual conferences in the not too distant future. My guess, however, is that this book will have to serve as a timely, and hopefully worthy, substitute.

On the other hand, I have an equally strong sense that private school parents will be much more receptive to my ideas about managing a private school than heads of schools and indeed administrators in general. My own experience suggests that parents have had serious concerns, at least many have had a vague sense of uneasiness for years, about the ever greater and ever more aggressive fundraising practices of most private schools, especially the wealthy, long-established ones located so prominently in New York City. Many parents are understandably suspicious of the lack of accountability when it comes to millions in annual giving, disappearing ambiguously under the convenient euphemism: *MIND THE GAP! between tuition and what it actually costs to educate a child*.

I am at the same time fairly confident that a large majority of trustees throughout the private school world also share many of my concerns, though here, too, largely remain silent in most cases in the face of such long-standing and accepted practices. After all, how do you begin to question practices that have worked so successfully for so long and are so dear to school administrators on every level and at every private school? It is understandably difficult and awkward, even for a trustee, much less parents, to raise these kinds of troubling questions. Nevertheless, for better or for worse, this little book now places these issues and concerns squarely on the table so to speak, in the hopes that a long-overdue discussion can finally take place—or, at a minimum, that they no longer remain ignored or simply wished away. My hope for this little book is that a serious discussion about fundraising and the proper management of private schools will finally take place, with parents, trustees, administrators, and faculty all participating on equal terms. And I hope the discussion can take place in an atmosphere largely free of the rancor and disapproval anticipated by the former director—and certainly without the exaggerated fear that one side or the other will be "strung up on the nearest oak!" After all, the organization he directed was the very type whose members should be welcoming such a debate in the first place. However, until that day arrives *in earnest*, I am fairly confident that the following prediction will unfortunately hold true:

This book will be disliked and unappreciated by private school heads and association directors in direct proportion to how much parents and trustees like and appreciate it.

WHAT GAP?

Our management philosophy of operating our school on tuition alone, and indeed, the underlying seed for this book, actually took root during my very first week at the helm, a period of time in the school's history far from any hint of success or celebration. It was during that hectic first week of school, as I now recall with a certain degree of wry amusement, that I was asked by the then-Director of Development to write the "annual fund appeal letter" for the 1981-1982 school year. Being new not only to Columbia Grammar and Prep School, but new to the private school world as such—not to mention knowing little about fundraising—I understandably needed help, and as it turned out, much more help than I could have ever imagined at the time.

Though I didn't know it during those early days, my almost total ignorance about any aspect of K-12 education, along with my ever-present Cartesian doubt, would end up being one of my most valuable assets. Not knowing anything led me to question everything. And one thing I questioned at the outset was the accepted notion of an annual fund.

What, I asked naively, was an annual fund?

"Oh," the development director replied, "that's what every school uses to close the gap between what tuition covers and what it actually costs to educate a student."

"Why is there a gap?" I asked.

She replied, "Every school has a gap between what parents pay and what it costs to run a school for a year."

Well, if I had been an experienced private school head, all this probably would have made good sense to me. And indeed, I would have written that first "annual fund appeal letter" with no questions asked. However, as I said, I was too ignorant and inexperienced in those early days to "know better," so to speak, and this "gap" business raised—stubbornly and persistently—all sorts of questions and doubts in my mind.

So, innocent as I was, I continued with my naïve questions: "When did this gap start?"

"There has always been a gap," replied my well-meaning and so very patient Director of Development.

"Always?" That Columbia Grammar would have started out in 1764 with a "gap" between tuition, on the one hand, and costs, on the other, seemed highly unlikely, even to my inexperienced ears. And if there was always a gap, then the so-called annual fund must have been there from the beginning as well. There must have been some point in the history of private education, I thought, let's say for talking purposes a hundred years ago, when the first private school came up with the clever idea of raising the money needed to close a deficit through voluntary giving—and lo and behold, the annual fund was born! Surely if no private school had ever faced a deficit, then there wouldn't have been any need for the creative idea of starting an annual fund. It certainly wasn't God-given or built into the fabric of private education. It had to have been, and surely was, a novel idea started by a single private school and ultimately adopted by all others including Columbia Grammar and Prep.

In any event, just when I was almost ready to put aside my philosophical skepticism, my patient development director said something that literally stopped me in my tracks. She explained to me that not only did a "gap" exist between tuition and the actual cost of educating a student but that this "gap" grew *larger* each year. That this was the case at Columbia Grammar and Prep School admittedly made some financial sense since we were in effect bankrupt and seemingly getting poorer by the year, but it was apparently also true at every other private school as well, according to her, even the very rich ones.

Now *there* was a fact to get any would-be philosopher thinking! It simply made no sense at all to me. Some of these private schools I knew to be quite solvent, with a history of success dating back hundreds of years. Moreover, they all charged more, some much more, in tuition than we did at that time and therefore had substantially more income to spend per child than we did. In addition, many of these very schools had millions in endowments, some had tens of millions, and the additional income to these schools must have been considerable—and growing yearly. So how then could these schools, the envy of any school head, conceivably have a "gap," much less one that was increasing each year?

Admittedly, as a newly minted headmaster with less than a week on the job, my lack of experience was getting a bit embarrassing, but while all this may sound quite commonplace and understandable to a seasoned private school head (or Director of Development, of course), to my untutored ears, it remained nevertheless quite a puzzle, raising far more questions than answers during that first week of school. And so my education began.

THE ANNUAL FUND "PITCH"

To appreciate fully what I have to say about annual giving, we must understand at the outset what is meant by an "annual fund" or "annual giving," terms that are interchangeable in the private school world. You would think that defining an annual fund would be a relatively easy task since virtually every private school in America has one. In fact, annual giving has become one of the sacred dogmas of private school financing, and every private school spends a lot of time and energy each year creating fancy annual fund brochures publicizing their appeals to parents and alumni, charitable foundations, as well as even to the many corporations that routinely support private schools through matching gift programs.

This is true not only of the many private schools in New York City, arguably the fundraising capital of the world, but true of private schools all across America. If you are, or ever have been, a parent in a private school, you know that an annual fund brochure will as surely find its way to your doorstep in early fall as the leaves will turn golden brown. Among private school parents there seems to be no way of resisting the push and lure of the annual fund, and with a resigned shrug of our shoulders, each year we take out our checkbooks and participate in one of the oldest and most respected rituals of the private school world: we donate to the annual fund.

Perhaps the easiest and most direct way to understand what annual giving is all about is to look at some actual examples of annual fund literature recently mailed from my cohorts right here in New York City, hot off the press so to speak. I see many annual fund brochures every year, all from quite wealthy K-12 schools, with large and growing endowments. They are among the oldest and most reputable schools to be found anywhere. And all are located, as I say, in New York City. However, it would not matter one bit if the brochures were in fact from struggling schools outside of New York with decrepit buildings and threadbare budgets. Indeed—and this begins to give you some insight into the peculiar nature of annual giving:

It makes no material difference whatsoever what type of private school the annual fund brochure comes from: rich or poor, large or small, K through 12 or elementary alone, old or new, town or country, urban or boarding, with a hefty tuition or a low tuition. In brief, no matter what type of school and no matter what condition it is in, financial or otherwise, with few variations in either language or style, the substance or "pitch" will always be the same.

And how could it possibly be that a "rich" school with high tuition and a bulging endowment has a *bigger gap* than a "poor" school with lower tuition and little to no endowment? It defied logic, not to mention common sense, to put it mildly. You can appreciate, therefore, why my suspicions were on high alert, even in those early years when I had no clear idea as to what might be going on!

The brochure from one school tells its constituency, parents and alumni, that:

Tuition revenue covers only about 80 percent of the cost of each student's education, leaving a gap of approximately $6,500 per student. The money raised through the annual fund helps the school to close this gap.

The Annual Fund is a vital source of support for [us].

The Annual Fund supports the day-to-day operations of the school.

The Annual Fund serves as a way for parents and alumni to advance the goals of our school.

And yet another school uses almost the identical language but with a slight variation:

The Annual Giving serves as a way for parents and alumni to advance the goals of our school, and the ongoing excellence of [our school] depends on your support of the annual fund.

Another school phrases its brochure somewhat differently:

The school's annual giving program provides the critical unrestricted support for the basic operation of the school—including faculty compensation and financial aid. Like all independent schools [our school] relies on three income sources to sustain its operating budget— tuition, income from endowment, and gifts to the annual fund.

This school goes on to make a critical admission, one that a good lawyer would never let it say in court for fear of incriminating itself:

In practical terms the annual giving program can be thought of as the school's checking account (money to be used in the current fiscal year for expenses) and the endowment as its savings account.

This is a key distinction that you will find at the core of virtually every private school's fundraising strategy or "pitch," namely that annual giving is for day-to-day purposes, namely the operating budget, while endowment funds are for long-range, namely, capital purposes. And as we will see further on, it is precisely because annual giving plays such an increasingly important role in a private school's *day-to-day* operations that it has now become more of a liability than an asset.

All schools emphasize in one way or another that annual giving—the school's "checking account"—makes improvements to the school and enhancements to the curriculum that would otherwise not be affordable:

Annual giving provides the support needed to offer a wide range of *improvements to the school*, from academic electives and lab equipment to increased faculty salaries.

The school may then go on to assure its parents that:

...*our reliance on tuition* to support our operations will be reduced by a strong annual fund.

Finally, the school makes this seemingly objective claim:

Only through the annual fund can tuition be kept as low as possible.

Of all the claims made for annual giving, the most universal and perhaps seemingly incontrovertible, is that tuition is *offset* or kept lower than otherwise to the extent that parents give money to a school voluntarily. For private, not-for-profit schools, this means donating to the annual fund. For private, not-for-profit colleges, it means donating to endowment funds. To repeat: *All not-for-profit schools, secondary and college, make the claim that voluntary giving offsets the costs of tuition.* I will challenge that claim—and all the others, for that matter—in the following pages.

And lastly, virtually all schools go on to emphasize an item that is often cited in annual fund appeal letters, namely, a dependency on the annual fund in order to improve financial aid. While not all schools mention this connection, some schools use the social and moral imperative of a "diverse school community" as the single most compelling rationale for giving to the annual fund. In this regard, such schools unabashedly go for the jugular vein by promising their constituencies that "dollar for dollar" all the proceeds from this year's annual fund will go toward scholarships to needy families the following year. In short, their annual fund campaigns represent a "double whammy," so to speak: On the one hand, the annual fund is touted as reducing tuition, something in everyone's self-interest, while on the other as providing scholarships to needy families at the now-reduced rate—all thanks to the generosity of the school's parent body. Given the huge size of some schools' annual fund "gap," it is understandable that a powerful marketing tool had to be found, and indeed, "helping needy families" and "promoting diversity" are about as persuasive as a school can get, after, of course, the universally shared goal of reducing tuition as much as possible.

Annual giving, as an enterprise, has become a major part of every private school's budget, not simply in terms of money, but of time and energy, as well. While 10 to 30 percent of a typical private school budget is represented by its annual fund, cumulatively, the private schools here in New York City raise approximately $100 million in annual giving alone, and well over $4 billion nationwide. A survey that crossed my desk recently gave a partial list of annual fund goals among private schools in New York City. Even I, inured as I have become to the ever-increasing amounts raised, was astonished to find a number of schools reporting that their "gaps" for the 2011-2012 school year were hovering around $10,000 and two over $13,000 per student—or more than 30 percent of their budgets. The annual fund, regardless of when or why it was originally conceived, has now become big business in the world of private education and has, by doing so, crossed the boundaries of what is both ethical and legal when it comes to using tax-deductible gifts.

HOT OFF THE PRESS

While excerpts from representative annual fund brochures and solicitations give you the essence of the typical annual fund "pitch," a more direct way to grasp the central role that the annual fund plays in the life (operating budget) of the average private school is to take a page out of the "playbook" of one of the better known private schools in our city. In a timely fashion, this counterpart of Columbia Grammar's, located just across Central Park, was kind enough to send me its latest annual giving report, with a number of pages devoted to this year's annual fund campaign. Here it is with slight variations and the name of the school tactfully changed to "The Other School," for purposes of discretion, though in reality there is nothing to hide. The Other School has not only sent its annual giving report to all its parents and alumni, which is standard practice, but to all other New York State Association of Independent Schools as well. The Other School, as it should be, is proud of its fundraising prowess and its Annual Report is professionally and technically quite impressive, as you can see from excerpts below:

The Other School

Please support the 2011-12 Annual Fund! With your generous help, our goal is to raise $4.2 million by June 30, 2012.

Why The Other School needs your help:

Tuition does not cover the entire cost of educating your child. Please help us close the gap of $10,700 per student for the 2011-12 school year.

Annual Fund gifts are critical to maintaining the quality of The Other School's overall program:

• Scientific equipment, trips, library books, and technology

• Improved compensation for our excellent and deserving faculty

- *Improved and expanded financial aid to promote a diverse school community*

- *Annual Giving offsets the cost of tuition for all families.*

The Other School simply cannot offer a comprehensive and highest quality education to your child without your voluntary gift to the Annual Fund.

Please help us close the gap through your generous support of the 2011-12 campaign for excellence. Thank you.

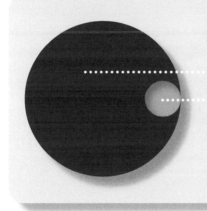

THE OTHER SCHOOL
Total per student cost $46,900

Gap: $10,700

Tuition and Fees: $36,200

While The Other School's annual fund appeal goes on for many pages, this one page gives you the heart and soul of every school's approach to annual giving. The knockout punch is the infamous pie chart, color coded and located front and center, the absolute substance and common thread found in literally every annual fund appeal: namely, that the tuition and fees well-meaning and hard-working parents pay to The Other School do not in reality cover the *full costs* of educating their children.

Now, if that doesn't make a self-respecting parent feel guilty, I don't know what will. In essence, The Other School is telling all their parents that if they don't pay $10,700 more in "voluntary giving" for each child enrolled over and above what they paid in tuition at the start of the year, then The Other School will not actually have enough money to carry out its full educational program—in brief, that its operating budget will not cover all its projected expense. Or, to put it in yet a different light, that The Other School cannot operate for the full year unless parents give—albeit on a "voluntary" basis—$10,700 per child to "close the gap!"

And, as if that's not guilt-inducing enough, The Other School goes on to point out on the opposite page some of the specifics of what "voluntary giving" would allow The Other School to do with all this charitable money, in effect to offer their students a full and comprehensive and indeed highest quality program. The Other School literally claims, without embarrassment or apology, that tuition and fees alone do not cover its already planned and promised program, the very program that presumably enticed prospective parents to choose The Other School over all other private schools in the first place! In brief, The Other School is literally saying in writing that it cannot provide The Other School students with a fullest and highest quality program on tuition alone and that without the additional "voluntary" contribution of $10,700 per student The Other School could not afford a range of items essential to its program. And here are just a few of those items that students over at The Other School would miss out on if the gap is not closed by generous contributions totaling $4.2 million for the year:

$55 provides a basketball for our varsity team.

$150 buys 15 copies of *The Elements of Style*.

$500 allows students to investigate and observe the life cycle of guppies in their classrooms.

$1,500 underwrites the lighting and set design for the Middle School musical.

$25,000 sends one of our classes to study shore ecology at a rustic nature center on the Maine coast, and so on.

The list of annual fund items that are dependent on "voluntary" gifts over and above tuition and fees is not very extensive in the brochure, but the poor parents over at The Other School are left with the impression that the list given is only part of a much longer list of items that their children will unfortunately have to forego unless the $4.2 million goal is reached.

Now, compare the situation over at The Other School with our own: Columbia Grammar provides all these enhancements to its academic program, and much more, all within the parameters of tuition alone, without, believe it or not, charging as much in tuition, on the one hand, or needing a single dollar in voluntary giving, on the other! Therein lies the core or essence of the question we are going to answer: How do we do so much more with so much less?

TRUTH IN ADVERTISING: OR, AT LEAST, FULL DISCLOSURE, PLEASE!

It has always struck me as strangely puzzling that more parents do not complain about the fact that private schools fail to disclose in any of their admissions literature or advertising what the "true costs" of educating a child in a given school actually are—costs that you soon hear all about only after the school year has started. And I am not here talking about the fact that more often than not, private schools charge thousands of dollars in fees: lunch, books, trips, music, lab, computer, insurance, etc., that are not included in the "tuition costs" listed in the admissions literature. Columbia Grammar, somewhat uniquely I might mention, has one inclusive "tuition charge" that comprises all of the above fees, plus much more, so that a parent at every grade level knows in advance of signing a contract exactly what a year of schooling at Columbia Grammar and Prep actually costs—with absolutely no surprises.

The fact that most other private schools, at least in New York City, do not routinely disclose all fees in their admissions brochures and literature is bad enough, but not disclosing the so-called "gap" is altogether worse, to my mind. Take The Other School as a case in point. While I haven't looked at their admissions brochures and related advertising, I will venture an educated guess that The Other School never mentions the astonishing fact that the so-called "real" cost of educating a child in The Other School will be tuition as advertised plus fees (not mentioned) plus the "gap," disclosed subsequently (only after the parent has signed the contract and his/her child has started school) at the tune of $10,700 per child over and above tuition!

Now, one would think that such a state of affairs would engender great upset and anger—at least, a lot of pointed questions—among parents who face such unexpected and undisclosed costs, after the fact, so to speak. However, quite to the contrary. Surprisingly, very few parents even raise an eyebrow over what would strike a consumer in any other financial area as a highly unacceptable business practice. Certainly, Verizon and AT&T wouldn't be allowed to get away with such an approach to financing their businesses. Hidden—or at least undisclosed—fees in any other area of commercial life are an absolute no-no. The private school world has its own special parameters as to what is or is not an acceptable business practice.

I suppose the obvious answer is simply that parents assume that the tuition costs initially listed by a school normally don't cover fees, as is true (except in our case), and that the "gap," though undisclosed as well, is nevertheless "voluntary," and not at all required. And while it is true that according to the IRS, a "voluntary, tax-deductible contribution" cannot be "required" as a matter of law, all schools, including The Other School, will do everything in their power—letters, personal solicitations, phonathons, etc.—all year long to get each and every parent to contribute a "voluntary" annual fund donation, which in The Other School's case, as we have pointed out, is a not-too-modest $10,700 per child. Most schools in New York City have "gaps" somewhere between $5,000 and $10,000 these days, though some reach gaps of over $13,000 for the 2011-2012 school year—and are climbing each year, I might add. In any respect, private school parents tolerate this otherwise deplorable situation, seemingly with a resigned shrug, and even more surprisingly, with a willingness to write the requisite check. Nevertheless, in my humble view, all schools should have to disclose for moral, if not legal, reasons, exactly what the financial expectations for a parent are in a given school far in advance of signing a contract. The admissions literature should clearly spell out the details: tuition, fees, and *expected voluntary gift to the annual fund*.

My suspicion is that not too many of my colleagues within the high-end private school world in New York City, certainly not The Other School, will embrace my suggestion that they be more forthcoming in disclosing in advance the size and nature of their "gaps" to their often unsuspecting parents. My guess is that as long as parents continue to acquiesce in this sleight of hand approach to annual giving, private schools will simply "leave well enough alone." But private schools should not be over-confident in this regard, because the rather alarming growth in the size of annual funds might well have reached a limit, what we have come to refer to these days as a "tipping point," and financially pressured parents just might start asking the requisite questions: For starters, where's all that money going, anyway?

HOW CAN A SELF-RESPECTING PARENT SAY NO?

New parents in a typical private school are likely to encounter one or more of four basic reasons for giving to the annual fund. It should be understood that while each school has its own unique way of expressing its case for annual giving, the "claims" or "reasons" always boil down to some combination of the following four.

ONE:

The Annual Fund reduces or offsets the costs of tuition by covering a portion of the operating costs in voluntary, tax-deductible dollars. In other words, every dollar given to the annual fund reduces tuition by a dollar, making the school more affordable and thereby closing the so-called "gap" between tuition and the "real" cost of a private school education.

TWO:

Perhaps the most commonly heard argument on behalf of annual giving centers on the straightforward appeal to parents for help in funding all those "extras" that collectively make a private school such a successful and attractive learning environment: more sports teams; more and better programs in the arts, theater and music; increased scholarships; improved teacher salaries and benefits; extra technology and updated lab equipment; and so on—not all of which can be covered by tuition alone. This rationale understandably resonates with every parent since the purported goal of annual giving will end up benefiting every child in the school, one's own very much included.

As one private school puts it, the annual fund is critical to its "ability to remain at the forefront of private education, not only in New York City, but throughout the country." In other words, tuition can only cover so much, but to be truly "excellent"—to truly offer the very best education to all the children—schools need voluntary giving beyond the costs of tuition itself. Indeed, as private schools never tire of repeating, the very success and well-being of a private school depends on that extra margin of support represented each year, at every private school, by the annual fund.

THREE:

The Annual Fund levels the playing field by making private education affordable to a wider range of families. By creating greater economic diversity within school communities, annual giving thereby encompasses an ethical as well as the purely practical goal of reducing tuition costs. In this direct way, tuition is therefore lower for everyone, a particularly appealing fact for those families with modest budgets. What could be clearer or more compelling, not simply from the strictly economic benefits involved, but from the social and ethical goal of including the broadest range of economic backgrounds in the school community? The greater affordability of a private education for families who would not otherwise be able to afford it is almost always cited by schools as the primary ethical reason for supporting the annual fund.

FOUR:

The Annual Fund is the only "legal" way to get financial support from the government by taking advantage of the tax-exempt status of private schools. Under 501(c)(3) of the tax code, anyone (parent, alumnus, or friend) who contributes to a school's annual fund is given an official school-stamped and signed receipt to be used on that year's tax returns, resulting in a tax rebate commensurate with the donor's tax bracket. In this way, of course, the donor is reducing tuition with tax-deductible dollars. To put it differently, the donor is getting a tax rebate from the government toward the costs of operating the school proportionate to the size of his/her gift and tax-bracket—a win/win situation for both parent and school.

At one point or another probably every private school parent wonders, "Wouldn't it be wonderful if our child's entire tuition could be paid in the form of a voluntary gift?"—in other words, in pre-taxed dollars. The same thought has probably occurred to every private school head as well. After all, your child's private school would have the same amount of money with which to operate if all the money came to it in the form of gifts and at the same time the parents would each get a 35 percent to 40 percent discount, depending on one's tax bracket, at least using typical New York City tax rates. In brief, what sensible-thinking parent would knowingly pass up the chance to pay for the largest possible portion—all, if it were legally possible—of their child's educational costs in tax-deductible dollars?

Unfortunately, two annoying IRS rules get in the way of allowing this mutually advantageous arrangement to cover the entire cost of tuition, in brief to cover the entire operating costs of a private school through tax-deductible donations. The IRS is quite clever when it comes to such arrangements and has long since made such a possibility illegal by issuing two IRS restrictions: (1) A tax-exempt organization, such as a private school, museum, public radio, etc., cannot charge or in any way require a *voluntary donation*. In other words, you cannot "charge" a donation, as you would tuition, and (2) A voluntary donation of any amount cannot be accepted on a tax-exempt basis by any tax-exempt organization in exchange for "goods and services."

In brief, a school cannot legally charge or require from parents a tax-deductible donation of any size, much less one that covered the entire costs of tuition for a child. In other words, a so-called "voluntary" donation must be just that—*voluntary*—and not in any way required, as are tuition and fees. And secondly, goods and services of any kind, large or small, cannot be paid for in pre-tax dollars—and tuition certainly covers a lot of goods and services.

These two IRS rules, taken together, raise all sorts of interesting questions about annual giving in general, but we should simply note at this point that the tax-deductibility of voluntary giving, whether ultimately legal or not, is a compelling marketing and financing tool available to tax-exempt private schools. Giving parents the ability or the option of paying part of their tuition in "pre-tax" dollars to cover the cost of their child's education is a powerful argument and an equally powerful incentive to give a "voluntary" donation to your child's school. For the average New York City private school parent, this would mean a welcome reduction in tuition costs of somewhere between 10 percent and 35 percent depending on what proportion of the operating budget the annual fund (purportedly) covers, but quite a lot of money per family each year when you consider that the average tuition among the K-12 schools is well over $30,000 per student. And that, in short, is why all private schools routinely begin each school year with an annual fund campaign based first and foremost on the hard-to-resist argument that the tax code allows a parent to pay some portion of tuition in tax-deductible dollars, thereby lowering tuition for all.

Most school heads would argue that any one of these four reasons alone would constitute sufficient justification for a school's annual giving program. However, even if you were inclined to quibble with one or more of these points, there is no question in anyone's mind that the four reasons taken together add up to a powerful rationale for annual giving. In one fell swoop, as they say in logic, a school can reduce the costs of tuition for its parents; it can pay for all the "extras" needed to make the school truly excellent and thereby provide the students with the finest possible education; it can make the school more affordable to a wider range of parents and therefore more diverse; and lastly, it can take advantage of its tax-exempt status by allowing parents to pay for a portion (ever larger in fact) of tuition with pre-tax dollars—all of this through the virtues of the annual fund. What a stroke of good fortune for private schools and their tuition-paying parents!

THE TRUTH, HOWEVER, IS OFTEN COUNTERINTUITIVE!

Unfortunately, the various rationales offered for the virtues of annual giving and how these funds improve and enhance private schools simply do not hold up under the light of day. In fact, there are good reasons for questioning all four of the most common rationales advertised by virtually all private schools in their annual fund brochures and literature.

Let's begin by looking at Claim #1, that annual giving *offsets the cost of tuition*. This is the most powerful and universal of all annual fund "pitches." Is it true? The claim seems quite logical, I admit, almost mathematically true at first glance. All the publicly available brochures—full of pie charts and graphs galore—clearly show that each school is charging less in tuition than the full costs of educating a child in that school, thanks largely to the generosity of parents through the annual fund, not to mention the often hefty income from endowment funds (voluntarily contributed by parents, as well, we should note). Can anything be clearer, therefore, than the "fact" that tuition is substantially lower than it otherwise would be, thanks to the income from both endowment and annual giving? Or, to put it somewhat differently, isn't it clear that the combined income from the annual fund and the endowment (if a school has one) is critical to a school's ability to cover its total annual costs—to close the "gap" between the total operating costs on the one hand and total tuition income on the other? Isn't that after all what every pie-chart ever published by any private school is precisely designed to show in a simple, pictorial format?

Well, appearances are often deceiving, or at a minimum, subject to varying interpretations. And nothing gets to the heart of a theoretical claim faster than a dose of reality. The fact is that wherever you find hefty endowments—and they range these days from $50 million to $125 million among the wealthiest private schools—you find comparably hefty tuitions!

Lo and behold, the facts do indeed point to an interpretation of annual giving—and endowment income, as well—quite at odds with the laudable claims found in the typical annual fund brochure, fancy pie charts and ethical claims notwithstanding. The first and most obvious conclusion to be drawn from this fact is that tuition costs are not the least bit reduced by annual giving and endowment income. In fact, the opposite seems to be true, namely, that the more a school raises in annual giving and the larger its endowment, the more it charges in tuition. These are the facts—with no exceptions in New York City, and I venture a gentleman's bet, with not more than a handful of exceptions elsewhere in America as well.

To get right to the point: Tuition costs simply do not respond to voluntary giving in the way schools advertise to their tuition-paying parents. No matter how large, how generous, or how consistent annual giving might be at a given school, tuition will not go down—or even *slow* down. Tuition costs grow independently of annual giving and are never therefore offset or influenced by the size or rate of annual giving. In short, they are both—annual giving on the one hand and tuition increases on the other—pushed forward by the same factors. Put differently, tuition increases and annual giving go up together—they work in tandem—and have no direct or causal connection.

This perplexing phenomenon is not only true for annual funds but for endowments as well. Endowment money is raised universally on the basis that the interest from endowments will serve, along with being available for a "rainy day," to offset the cost of tuition, just as annual giving supposedly does. Pie charts, although in a simplistic manner, always point this out. Whenever a school has an endowment, a certain percentage of endowment income is dutifully shown, and indeed ultimately spent, as part of the operating budget of a private school, not to mention every college and university in America—indicating, as logic would lead you to believe, that endowment income is *offsetting* some of the costs of educating your child in that school. (Harvard, by the way, claims that 42 percent of its operating budget is covered by income from its $36 billion endowment, while Princeton claims an astounding 45 percent, the largest percentage for any university in America. Need I point out that both have among the highest tuitions in America as well?) The fact is a school's endowment can grow beyond a school's wildest dreams (Harvard, Yale, and Princeton) and will never—in spite of what is claimed—offset, or decrease, or control in any way whatsoever the cost of tuition. Again, simply put, the very factors in any private school that drive up the costs of tuition are the very factors that necessitate the need for greater and greater fundraising, whether it's annual giving or endowment income.

One would think, again naïvely, that whenever and wherever you find large endowments and large annual funds, you will surely find smaller tuitions. The fact is, however, that nothing could be further from the truth. On the contrary, the larger the endowments and the larger the annual giving, the larger the tuitions. And even more telling than that revealing relationship is the fact that tuitions and annual giving not only grow larger together, but do so at basically the same rate. If you do a survey of New York City schools alone, you can rank them by tuition, rank them by endowment, or rank them by annual giving—their respective size as well as rate of growth—and the rankings come out the same no matter which one of the criteria you use.

The fact is, large endowments, large annual funds, and large tuitions all go hand in hand. What the naïve, unsuspecting, well-intentioned, and generous parent was led to believe, that writing a check to the endowment or giving a check to the annual fund would offset the cost of tuition, is not at all true, superficial appearances notwithstanding. If Adam Smith's "impartial spectator" were to cast his objective gaze upon the world of private school finances, he would have to conclude, based on overwhelming empirical evidence, that large endowments in conjunction with large annual funds *lead* to large tuitions, and not at all the opposite as claimed. Protestations to the contrary, the fact is the more money you give to a school, the more money is spent, and the faster you give it, the faster it is spent—meaning ever higher, not lower, tuitions.

So it seems we are faced at the outset with a logical oddity: what seemed at first so simple and straightforward in actual fact only makes sense if you read it in the opposite way intended—in brief, you must literally stand Claim #1 on its head. You must, contrary to the comfortable assurances made in just about every private school's annual fund brochure, come to the very different conclusion that *large endowments and large amounts of annual giving serve to drive up the costs of tuition*, not, as the argument goes, keep tuition as low as possible. Odd and unlikely as this conclusion might appear, there simply is no denying it once you look beyond the laudable claims of annual fund brochures and more closely at the facts of how private schools (and colleges) in reality operate.

So we need to figure out why private schools, particularly the more rich and successful they are, become ever more dependent—and not less—on deficit spending, in other words, on voluntary giving to balance their budgets. Why is it, therefore, that the private schools with the highest and fastest growing tuitions, the largest and fastest growing endowments, and the largest and fastest growing annual funds are the very schools that have the largest and fastest growing "gaps" between tuition income and "what it actually costs to educate a child"?

FOLLOW THE MONEY

To make concrete sense of this bizarre situation, to figure out what in fact drives up the cost of tuition on the one hand, and why on the other hand voluntary giving seems to have no discernible impact on these costs, we need to look now at Claim #2: Voluntary giving allows a school to make improvements that it otherwise could not afford through tuition income alone. In brief, while tuition per se might not in fact get reduced through voluntary giving, tuition costs are nevertheless kept lower than they would otherwise be by virtue of the "fact" that all sorts of improvements and en-hancements to the academic and extracurricular life of the school can and are in fact purchased with annual fund dollars—instead of tuition dollars. Tuition might not be lower, but the school is a lot better off due to annual giving—or so it is claimed, literally by every private school in America.

Most parents who bother thinking about these issues—namely the comparative costs of tuition among private schools, the relative size of a given school's endowment, and the amount of voluntary giving in recent years—will naturally assume that the schools charging more in tuition, raising more in annual giving, and those with larger endowment incomes are *ipso facto* spending more money per child. To the extent private school parents might think seriously about such questions, which is probably not often or in any depth, they most likely come to the conclusion that you are paying more at a more expensive school to get more. After all, isn't that basically true of most areas of life: restaurants, diamonds, tickets to the opera, etc. And furthermore, where else would all that "extra" money from heftier tuitions, large annual funds, and big endowments go, if not towards each child's education in a given school? This is precisely what every annual fund brochure claims or certainly implies in so many words, and it certainly makes perfectly good sense to assume that all these claims are basically true.

Well, what's true is the first part—that *more* money is indeed being spent at those schools charging more in tuition and raising more money in voluntary giving as well, with large infusions of endowment income to boot. What is *not* true, unfortunately, is that this "extra money" is being spent on your child, or on any child in those schools. It is being spent, but not how you as a parent would expect or want it to be spent—on the students, which is to say, in the academic areas in general. Could such a harsh and sweeping indictment of private school fundraising possibly be true—even somewhat true? Well, let's have a closer look.

If not on the students, where then do all these well-funded private schools spend the "extra" thousands of dollars they receive each year in annual giving? To find out, let's take as our example one of these otherwise unnamed rich schools, which we will continue to call The Other School. The Other School, located right here in New York City, claims to spend $10,700 more per student per year than Columbia Grammar—it's what they literally say in their latest annual fund brochure. But keep in mind, as we try to answer all these questions about annual giving and costs per student, that this actual Other School we are comparing Columbia Grammar to, charges more than we do in tuition, has a much larger endowment, and is asking each parent to give—albeit voluntarily—over $10,700 on average for each child enrolled to cover their "gap." On the other hand, Columbia Grammar has only negligible endowment income, charges less per child in tuition, and has no annual fund—period. Is The Other School therefore spending *more* money—indeed, *much more* money—per student than we are on such essentials as teacher salaries and benefits, on library books, on computers and science equipment, on reading and math specialists, on theater and art, on physical education and competitive sports? It would clearly seem so, for after all, where would all that "extra" money be going otherwise?

While I promise to provide a clear and unambiguous answer to this question, I must, however, caution the reader at the outset that the answer to this and similar questions will be somewhat circuitous and at times difficult, if not frustrating to follow. The problem is that we simply do not have access to the operating budgets of other private schools. If we did, we could answer such questions with a brief and straightforward analysis, comparing our operating budget line by line with another private school's.

MIND THE GAP!

Unfortunately, such a direct approach is not available to us. Anyone who has spent any time in the private school world, whether as a parent, teacher, trustee or administrator, knows quite well that a private school budget is a closely guarded secret and is treated with as much confidentiality as the Swiss banking system. Heaven forbid that we should ever expose our respective budgets to the light of day! For my part, I would be more than happy to compare—publicly or otherwise—our detailed budget with any other private school's in New York City. However, to my knowledge, nothing remotely near this level of sharing has ever taken place—or in all likelihood, will ever take place—in the private school world. And believe me, I've asked enough of my fellow heads to know that first of all they will say "no" with not a moment's further consideration and that second of all they will henceforth look at me as someone akin to a KGB spy out to destroy the very fabric of private education, premised as it is on arcane accounting and shrouded in confidentiality. Indeed, a private school's budget is not even shared with the tuition-paying parents in a particular school, much less with other competitive private schools.

Perhaps some day, Julian Assange and WikiLeaks will publish all those "secret" private school budgets on the Internet. However, until that happens, by necessity, we must find another way of comparing Columbia Grammar's operating budget with the operating budgets of the private schools that have those impressively large annual funds each and every year, with equally impressive endowments waiting in the wings—in brief, the better known and more reputable private schools in New York City, of course! The only other way to answer our questions, the only other way to get to the heart of the matter, will involve a much more circuitous route and will require a lot more creativity on our part, and a bit more patience as well, than many readers might be willing to spare. Nonetheless, I promise that, in spite of a few extra detours and a little added complexity here and there, the journey will end up being every bit as successful, and perhaps somewhat more interesting, than a more straightforward comparison. After all, any subject as dry and seemingly uninviting as "private school management and finances" ought to be spiced up with a little in-

120

trigue to make our journey truly worth the effort.

By necessity, therefore, our approach will involve a more general comparison of facts and figures made publicly available by other private schools themselves in such publications as annual giving reports, the 990 Forms required by the IRS, fundraising literature sent routinely to parents and alumni, and the like. While these public documents are expressly designed to convey as little worthwhile information as possible through the use of pie charts and the like, the reader will nevertheless be surprised by how much helpful information we can glean from all these various sources if we look carefully enough and read between the lines, so to speak. In the end, we can still reach our destination—namely to understand once and for all the true role of the infamous private school "gap," the so-called gap between tuition costs and what it supposedly costs to educate a child in a specific school—best of all, where all that "gap" money actually ends up!

So while we cannot simply compare budgets and thereby resolve our questions straightforwardly, we can nevertheless make an "educated" guess as to where and how The Other School, for example, is spending all those thousands of extra dollars per student. The next best thing to actually comparing our budgets, apples to apples, is to compare two schools, The Other School, on the one hand, and Columbia Grammar and Prep, on the other, from the point of view of open-minded parents shopping for the best school for their children.

Put simply, if The Other School is operating on a total of about $10,700 more per student each year than we are, then you would think that The Other School would exhibit some rather glaring benefits and improvements over our school. Certainly, if Columbia Grammar were to have at its disposal some $10,700 more per student to spend next year than tuition alone provides—an overnight increase of approximately 26 percent in our operating expenditures for the same number of students—every parent, student, and teacher would recognize the improvements the first day of school.

Let's see, then, if we can readily recognize the significant benefits that The Other School has to offer over our school if we look at both schools simply from a broad consumer's point of view. Let's put ourselves in the familiar role of the many thousands of parents who every year shop for the very best private schools for their sons and daughters.

AN EDUCATED CONSUMER

Fortunately for Columbia Grammar, the overwhelming majority of parents are, as Sy Syms, the clothing magnate and philanthropist, famously put it, "educated consumers." When shopping for a private school, an educated consumer will look for small classes (which is reflected in a low student/faculty ratio), a comprehensive and challenging academic program, excellent and well-maintained facilities, excellent teachers, extensive programs in the arts, and a varied and inclusive sports program.

Every fall, parents by the many thousands compare the "educational value" of the various schools on their lists, and no parent, to my knowledge, has ever found Columbia Grammar lacking in such a comparison. On the contrary, parents touring our school can readily see that our classes are smaller on average, with a 6.7/1 student/faculty ratio, easily among the lowest in the city—and therefore among the *most expensive*; our buildings are newer and better maintained—and therefore *more expensive*; our starting teacher salaries are higher—and therefore *more expensive*; our art, music, and theater programs are more extensive, with more full- and part-time teachers per student—and therefore *more expensive*; our competitive sports programs are more extensive and more heavily staffed—47 teams and 76 coaches—and therefore *more expensive*; seven (soon to be eight) modern science labs with four Intel semi-finalists over the last 10 years—and therefore *more expensive*; and finally we have more square footage per student (and therefore *more expensive* to build, furnish, clean, and maintain) than you can find at The Other School. The many other areas of concern, such as libraries, theaters, gyms, cafeterias, the lunch program itself (all natural foods which are *more costly*), school trips, and the like, surpass or, at a minimum, compare favorably not only with The Other School but with any other private school in New York City.

So the "proof is in the pudding" for all to see in a tangible and indisputable way: Columbia Grammar and Prep School spends as much or more on a student's education than any private school in New York City, *bar none*—and we do it without needing a dollar in annual giving or endowment income, for that matter; we do it on tuition alone. This is a fact, and if any private school wishes to challenge this claim, I am more than willing and available—you could even characterize it as eager—to compare our respective budgets line by line, dollar for dollar, tomorrow. And if not tomorrow, whenever you can convince one of the many fine K-12 schools in the city to accept my open invitation.

Even though our broad comparison of schools is far less satisfactory than a detailed budget comparison would be, what we know at this point is that annual giving and endowment income are *not* being spent on *improving education* or *reducing tuition* over at The Other School—the two main reasons The Other School and virtually all other private schools regularly give to justify their annual giving campaigns. By default then, The Other School must be spending its extra $10,700 per student per year *outside* the academic area. Where then do we turn to find our answer as to where exactly all that money is being spent? Well, to be truthful, there aren't too many "non-academic" areas in a school budget. So, if we look at one last clue, I think that we can begin, finally, to solve our mystery.

THE TELEOLOGY OF OVER-SPENDING

This last clue comes straight from The Other School's annual fund brochure and leads us directly to the heart of private school overspending, or to characterize it more accurately, *misspending*, especially at those schools that have large annual funds—and even more so when those annual funds are combined with large endowments. The Other School's brochure states that it likes to *"think of the annual fund as a checking account."*

Voila! What extraordinary good fortune to have such an "unrestricted checking account" filled to the brim—over $4 million annually and steadily growing, to be exact—with the privilege of spending it in any way one wishes within the broad concept of "general operating expenses."

Now you can just imagine if you were the CEO of a business enterprise, which all private schools are, of course, and your board of directors told you not to worry about balancing your budget since the board, with annual contributions from stockholders and customers, was generously making available to you an overdraft checking account that would allow you to cover any expenditures that might exceed your annual budget. Surely you would end up overspending, or as we more correctly noted, misspending all that money. Indeed, your overdraft checking option would undoubtedly become a *license to overspend*.

Aristotle, in his great wisdom, called this kind of "cause and effect" relationship "teleological." It is the comfort and reassurance that you can spend all you want with no adverse consequences that *causes* you to overspend. In a similar vein, excessive worry, for example, might well cause someone to have a heart attack, though no amount of searching during the autopsy would ever find such a cause. A teleological cause doesn't cause things to happen in the normal, straightforward, physical sense of cause, but nevertheless the event in question, in this case overspending by private schools (or anxiety heart attacks in people), would not have happened had the teleology of the circumstances—in other words, the teleological causes—not existed. And it goes without saying that if Aristotle were miraculously to return to our world as an educational consultant he would have a field day addressing the teleology of annual giving. Annual fund teleology always leads in one direction, and one direction only—overspending. Over any length of time, this very bad habit of overspending becomes the even worse habit of misspending.

To put the matter in the most straightforward light, the overdraft checking aspect of annual giving becomes ingrained thinking for every headmaster sooner or later, usually sooner, and becomes a license to overspend. Rather than figure out what a school actually ought to and can prudently spend at the beginning of the year (and there's no better parameter in the world than tuition income itself), spending gets determined by tuition income *plus whatever additional amount can be raised*, in other words, the money available, which is code in the private school world for "tuition income plus annual giving plus endowment income."

The thought of living on tuition income alone is simply not considered a viable option these days among private school heads, and even to broach the subject is tantamount to labeling yourself an outsider or worse, a naïve country bumpkin. Those responsible for running private schools believe without question that annual giving and endowment income are not only vital but essential to the viability and quality of their respective schools, when in reality nothing could be further from the truth—such is the pernicious influence of the "teleological mind-set" on the management of schools today.

New York City in particular has become a veritable land of milk and honey for many years now—at least as far as fundraising within the private school world is concerned—and has provided the perfect "teleological environment" for increasing annual giving on a seemingly limitless basis. Private school heads in particular are perfectly well aware of this open invitation to raise unrestricted funds—to fatten their "overdraft checking accounts"—and therefore to spend largely without the usual kinds of financial anxieties or reservations that budgeting would normally entail. Hence, school budgets invariably become loaded with unnecessary spending, and thus the inevitability in turn of an ever-increasing, ever-larger annual fund.

While in the direct sense school headmasters are the primary culprits in this management scenario, it is nevertheless the boards of trustees who routinely—and surprisingly—give their wholehearted blessing to what we might politely refer to as the "culture of overspending." Even where boards raise an occasional word of concern about this ever-increasing appetite for deficit spending, little if anything is ever done to slow its growth. It has always struck me as a source of great puzzlement that boards, comprised as they are in large part of parents and alumni who are by definition successful in business, law, medicine, and similar careers requiring considerable discipline, do not expect the same degree of discipline from school heads. I suppose it has something to do with the fact that school heads are "academics" first and foremost in the eyes of board members and therefore are to be judged on different standards. Second only to religious leaders, perhaps, school heads are given a degree of latitude that few others entrusted with such large amounts of money are similarly accorded.

Whatever the answer, the fact remains that boards of trustees surprisingly condone large scale "deficit spending" when it comes to private schools, whereas, I would venture to guess, they would naturally refuse to tolerate it in other areas, their own private businesses, or their own household budgets, for that matter. While it is thoroughly understandable and appropriate that boards follow a "hands-off" policy in regards to the instructional program or academic administration and policy, no such carte blanche, in my view, should be extended to non-academic staffing and finances. What better way is there, after all, for trustees to exercise their fiduciary responsibilities than to ask the awkward but essential questions as to how a school's voluntary gifts are being spent? And this is precisely the question we will answer when it comes to The Other School's annual fund of $4.2 million, generously given to the school by parents, trustees and alumni.

THE BLACK HOLE

There is no need to beat around the (academic) bush looking for where the annual giving money goes: the black hole of spending lies squarely in the domain of *administration*. That's where all or most of a school's "gap" money, which is provided by the annual fund, goes, year in and year out. However, whenever I suggest anything along these lines to a fellow head of school, I invariably elicit howls of protest. The main objection—and this is true of *every* head I have spoken to about my views— is that no amount of cutting of administrative expenses could conceivably result in sufficient savings to close the "gap" in their respective operating budgets without the considerable help of an annual fund.

For example, The Other School would need to cut about $4.2 million out of its operating budget to achieve a balanced budget without the help of its annual fund, a sum seemingly out of reach based solely on cost-cutting and the like. I am certain that the headmaster of The Other School would think that finding $4 million in extra or unneeded administrative staff and related types of waste would be totally out of the question. And while most private schools admittedly have smaller "gaps," some have substantially larger gaps than The Other School. As I mentioned previously, some of my cohort schools have "gaps" per student of over $10,000, some over $13,000, according to their own published reports. Their cumulative deficits per year, in some cases, therefore total over $5 million, a staggering sum even on inflated New York City terms. It is no wonder, therefore, that the typical head completely dismisses my claim that waste in the administrative area can easily and straightforwardly account for virtually all the so-called "gaps" in their respective budgets.

I admit that it probably should strike the reader as somewhat farfetched as well. What school, after all, consciously believes that it has excess administrative positions, duplication of duties, or other types of obviously wasteful habits? To be sure, the overwhelming majority of private schools are managed with the best of intentions, mindful in large part at least of the issues of waste and duplication.

Most heads think that if I'm not simply joking, I am at least ignorant of the virtues and importance of their respective administrative structures. Cutting any of their administrative positions, at least as much as 4-5 million dollars worth, would most certainly damage their ability to carry out their missions and provide their students, families, and faculty with the appropriate support they need. In brief, none of my fellow school heads has ever taken me seriously, much less taken me up on the "friendly" offer I always make, to find, as a *pro bono* gesture, waste and duplication in their administrative hierarchy *equivalent* to the amount of money they are attempting to raise during the year in annual giving.

At this point in our conversation, my fellow school heads inevitably reject my offer as totally preposterous, not to mention downright disparaging of their own considerable abilities to manage the school in question. I counter by asking these skeptical heads to conduct with me a hypothetical exercise to resolve the question in a straightforward fashion. I ask them to imagine, for the moment, that I am the newly appointed president of their boards of trustees, and I am asking—ordering to be exact—that $4 million be cut from their operating budgets for the following year. The exercise is to determine how one would go about finding, and then cutting, the equivalent of one's annual fund goal from one's operating budget.

This, then, is the hypothetical test I ask my colleagues to pass—regardless of how "impossible" such a task might at first appear, or how insulting they feel the test is in the first place. The fact is, I always assure my disbelieving colleagues, that if their respective boards were in fact to decide tomorrow to require them to cut the equivalent of their schools' annual funds in expenses for the next school year, it could surely be done—*and without harm to their academic program*! I will make a gentleman's wager here and now with any head of any school in New York City that it can be done—as long as the endowment at the school in question is as large or larger than the annual operating budget, which is true for most of the better known K-12 schools in New York City. At schools where the endowment is less than the operating budget, the amount of waste is equivalent to that smaller ratio. Hence a school whose endowment is equal to half its operating budget would be wasting approximately half its annual fund, and so on.

No headmaster has actually taken me up on this offer, my *pro bono* gesture notwithstanding. Nevertheless, to all those disbelieving and reluctant heads out there, I offer The Other School as a representative test case, and ask you to follow our thought process as we seek to cut more than $4 million from The Other School's budget, as a case in point. A few simple steps will invariably guide us directly to the areas where significant savings can be found.

Where should the headmaster turn to eliminate The Other School's "gap" of $4 million? Well, the first and most obvious solution to a balanced budget is to raise tuition. Something on the order of a 15 percent tuition increase would just about close the "gap" and leave The Other School with a balanced budget. However, there's an obvious problem with that solution, of course. If The Other School raises tuition too much too rapidly, it may have a hard time remaining competitive—and would probably lead to the board's dismissal of the headmaster for that reason alone. Consequently, closing the "gap" through a larger than usual tuition increase is simply not an option. The only alternative is to cut costs. But $4 million? Surely that would be impossible.

To cut costs of such a magnitude, the headmaster might be tempted to then turn to the academic area because, after all, it constitutes by far the largest proportion of the budget. He realizes that simply increasing class size (raising the student/faculty ratio) might be a solution. Because his annual faculty payroll is somewhere around $20 million, a 20 percent increase in the student/faculty ratio would just about cover the $4 million and balance his budget without the need of an annual fund to close a "gap" in the operating budget. By necessity, some teachers would, unfortunately, have to be cut and openings due to retirement, family leave, or non-reappointment would also have to go unfilled, but the task of saving $4 million would have been accomplished—or largely so—and the headmaster's job would be saved in one step, albeit a painful one.

But once again, the headmaster realizes that there are serious problems with this approach. Not only would all these layoffs and cuts demoralize the faculty—who have in all likelihood never experienced any such cost cutting in their private school tenures—but the increase in student load would cause, at least in the eyes of faculty and parents, a decline in quality. Moreover, there is the realistic concern that The Other School could no longer compete successfully with the likes of Columbia Grammar with an already *lower* student/faculty ratio. Therefore, any increase in faculty workload of this magnitude or increase in the student/faculty ratio would surely be a competitive "kiss of death." So that approach will not work, either.

The now worried and clearly perplexed headmaster might next consider cutting back on maintenance and cleaning. While these areas are not a very large part of the operating budget, significant savings could perhaps be achieved if drastic cuts, perhaps just for one year, were made in cleaning, along with a one-year moratorium on maintenance needs. But again all he has to do is look at his competitors, Columbia Grammar in particular, to see that any lack of cleanliness or signs of disrepair would put The Other School at a great disadvantage in the admissions process, with all those daily tours of parents scrutinizing every nook and cranny of the school. Word would quickly get back to the board, and the headmaster would rightfully get fired under such circumstances. Consequently, the headmaster must once again look elsewhere for savings.

Similarly, the sports programs and student activities, such as the music, theater, and arts programs, can't be cut either, for similar reasons. New York City parents are the first to notice and to protest any cutbacks in the arts. Any reduction in the arts would most certainly prove disastrous in the highly competitive admissions process among New York City private schools. In brief, the headmaster over at The Other School must, out of competitive necessity, look outside the academic areas and indeed outside of any area that would weaken the instructional program and extracurricular activities.

Where does he turn now? The only remaining area that could be cut at this point involves strictly administrative positions and the space, supplies, and related costs of supporting those positions. Could $4 million, or any figure approximating that princely sum, possibly be cut from administrative positions alone? It seems highly unlikely, and certainly the headmaster of The Other School doubts that it can be done without bringing the school to a screeching halt.

Well, we have come this far in our hypothetical exercise, so let's take this very last step anyway, however impractical our task might appear at this point. Our hypothetical headmaster must find a way to live within those constraints and at the same time keep the school running efficiently and successfully. Well, in spite of our headmaster's stubborn resistance and skepticism, cutting an amount in administrative costs equivalent to the $4 million "gap" is nevertheless perfectly doable at any school the size of The Other School. How can I be so confident? As odd as it sounds, the fact that The Other School has such a large annual fund, totaling as it does $4 million, combined with a large endowment, larger in total than its operating budget for the year, is a sure clue that it is wasting similarly large sums in unnecessary positions and expenses in the administrative area.

I sum up this conclusion in something I refer to as the "Fundamental Principle of Private School Management," which states: *At any private school where the endowment is as great or greater than the operating budget (all the best known schools), the amount of waste each school produces each year is equivalent—at a minimum—to its annual fund.* This principle says, in effect, that *every school with a large endowment is ipso facto wasting the equivalent of its annual fund in administrative overhead.* Keep in mind that I am mostly speaking here of the relatively "wealthy" private schools, those with substantial endowments and large annual funds supplementing their operating budgets, which are already well-supported through their larger than average tuition costs. As I noted earlier, however, the Fundamental Principle applies to all schools, but at schools where the endowment is less than the operating budget, the amount of waste is equivalent to that smaller ratio.

My principle is based on years of observation. Every private school I have had the opportunity to visit has an overstaffed business office, maintenance department, development office, and most certainly an administrative hierarchy far too cumbersome and duplicative to serve any constructive purpose. If I run across another school with a director or associate head of institutional advancement and planning, or a director of strategic planning, or layers of assistant and associate headmasters, I will despair that our private schools will ever balance their budgets without an annual infusion of tax-deductible dollars over and above tuition. What after all is the school headmaster doing if not "planning and advancing" the institution? And it is hard to find a school large or small, but certainly one the size of Columbia Grammar, that does not have one, two, three, or even four associate heads for various areas of responsibility (what are the heads of the divisions doing?) to a whole range of administrative functions that operate independently at those schools but could be more efficiently carried out under one person/title/salary. It is not just the unnecessary salaries that burden a school, but the inefficiency of over-staffing that leads to such waste of both time and money.

The business offices of our brother and sister schools in New York City, especially those of comparable size, but even those much smaller, have anywhere from six to 10 staff (one has 13), their development offices are comparably large, and their financial aid, buildings and grounds, strategic planning, curriculum, etc. are often separately staffed as well. There is an extraordinary amount of duplication of duties cozily living side by side in their administrative set-ups. Some of the schools, I discovered, even have a comptroller! As former Mayor Ed Koch might have exclaimed, "Gimme a break!" Who, after all, could be a better comptroller than the Chief Financial Officer? It's inconceivable to me that the CFO needs a comptroller or that the CFO's job can be made easier, better, more efficient, or helped in any way whatsoever by this additional person/position. You don't need two people doing a job in a complicated and complex way when one person can handle the very same responsibilities in a straightforward, simpler way.

Our Chief Financial Officer not only directs our finances but controls them quite well to boot. Besides, as I mentioned, he serves as our financial aid officer and our "facilities coordinator" as well, which, by the way, was yet another "new" job I found at a number of schools that was handled by a separate and expensive staff. One of these "comptroller" schools also had a "payroll benefits" person (don't ask me how that could conceivably be a separate position, much less a full-time one, which it was), and all three schools had from five to nine more staff in the business office alone than we do. Add to this such high-level positions as Director of Diversity, a responsibility we all should and do have on a full-time basis that in no way, in my humble opinion, should be delegated to a separate individual or department—which inevitably leads to more separation and division—rather than inclusion and a greater sense of community.

Director of Public Relations is also in vogue at a number of the schools the size of Columbia Grammar or smaller—and as I already asked rhetorically, who other than the head of school should direct public relations? And one of my recent favorites, Director of Human Resources, a position I won't even begin to try to define, though I do vaguely recall some such position from my distant college days. There are no doubt other equally "essential" administrative positions waiting to be discovered through more research on my part, but these should suffice to indicate how far from immune our private schools have become to the bureaucratic "culture" of separation of duties and duplication of tasks. And please don't forget all those extra secretaries!

Recently, I was invited for a live interview by a radio talk-show host who was particularly interested in the subject of "administrative bloat," and in the course of our conversation he asked me to give the most "glaring" comparison of our approach with another school's. I immediately thought of Joyce, our bursar, as the best example of how we manage to keep our administrative costs to a minimum, especially compared to some of the high-end private schools in New York City.

Bursar, as you might know, is simply an old-fashioned name for the person who is responsible for collecting tuition from parents, whether in a private secondary school or college. Joyce has been our bursar for three decades, and in those early days, she collected somewhere around $900,000 a year. Gradually, as we survived insolvency and under-enrollment, the school began to prosper, slowly but surely, and tuition grew as well. And when we had the good fortune to open our new high school building in the fall of 1985, enrollment and, accordingly, our finances grew exponentially. One spring Joyce came to see me with an understandable request: she needed help.

As she explained it, she had started out collecting $900,000 a year with a much smaller number of parents to deal with. However, by the fall of 1986 or 1987, she was collecting well over $3 million!

I replied that her request seemed perfectly reasonable, and that we would look for a person to help her out right away. But first, I suggested the following proposition: How about if I give you a couple thousand over the automatic raise we are all getting in a few months, and in turn you try to handle the office for just one more year on your own.

Well, Joyce liked the idea and off she went with a pretty tidy increase for the following year. In fact, I did not hear from her for about three to four years, if I recollect correctly, perhaps even a bit longer. But, inevitably and understandably, Joyce showed up again in my office. After all, we were becoming a popular choice, finally, among New York City parents, and tuition income was growing exponentially. And yes, the conversation went more or less as before. We were then up to $7.5 to $8 million, and it certainly seemed time, as I readily agreed, to find Joyce a capable assistant. Nevertheless, when I offered her a few more thousand to try it on her own just one more year, Joyce accepted the challenge—and of course another nice boost in salary.

When we eventually got up to $15 million after the middle school building was built in the 1990s, Joyce was understandably in my office once again—and ditto: She once again made a plea for an assistant but once again accepted the challenge of "just one more year" and of course yet another salary boost.

Well, by now you know how the story goes. We are today over $50 million in tuition income, and yes, Joyce is still collecting it all on her own, with what the auditors tell me is the smallest uncollectible amount among the private schools in the city, usually less than $10,000 though always under $25,000—on over $50 million in collectibles! And lest you think Joyce is an unhappy, overworked member of our staff, the very contrary is true. Except for some crunch times when tuition is due, Joyce is one of the most relaxed—certainly best paid—bursar you will find anywhere, and someone who claims to have the best and most enjoyable job in the world.

And as far as comparisons are concerned, I amusedly compare our bursar's office with that of one of our primary competitors, a school of comparable size and scope, and therefore of comparable tasks for our respective bursars. This school, I have been recently informed, has nine full-time staff collecting roughly the same amount of tuition! In brief, this school has eight additional people, or roughly $750,000 more in salary and benefits than we spend in just one office—not to mention more space being wasted, more turnover and therefore hiring and firing, more inter-staff conflicts, more trash and coffee spilled, and so on. And as you will see in the next chapter, when a more comprehensive survey and analysis of a school (or college/university) is done, the cumulative waste is staggeringly large, in many cases equivalent to the annual fund itself. For me personally, Joyce has always served as proof positive that when it comes to bureaucracies, the old adage has never been more valid: "Less is always more."

These unnecessary positions are the hidden costs in private schools. No one is quite sure what these sorts of "extra" administrators do or what precise purposes they serve. My guess is that they exist in a sort of protected vacuum, sort of the way I also assume that the many White House as-sistants and advisors exist—which is to say, hidden from public view until some scandal or another occurs—and more or less at the discretion and on the good faith and credibility of the president. Indeed, we rightfully ought to give presidents and heads of school the "benefit" of the doubt. They indeed ought to have some degree of latitude and independence to surround themselves with administrators who will assist them in doing the very best job possible. That is all fine and good, and certainly understandable from the point of view of the typical board of trustees trying to show its support and belief in the good judgment of the head of school.

However, what is to be done when that headmaster starts wasting money on a bloated and needlessly expanding administration? Indeed, the "mother of all waste and duplication" can always be found just outside the headmaster's office. Saying this, of course, will surely cost me the last of my "friends" among my colleagues, assuming I have any left, but here I go anyway. At virtually any school, but definitely at any school with a large and growing annual fund, the biggest amount of waste, inefficiency, and costs comes in the form of associate and assistant heads and their support staff.

Either I have foolishly missed out on something all these years or I am now boasting—take your pick—but I started out 30 years ago with a very small school run by one headmaster (myself) assisted by one secretary/assistant (same person) and here we are today with the same two people running a school that is three times the size in population and many more times larger in physical size and financial complexity. We manage quite well, and I have yet to figure out what a third, much less a fourth or fifth, person might do besides get in the way. While I don't know what all these additional staff are supposedly accomplishing, I do know that together all these additional positions and support staff add up to a small fortune in non-academic spending. It doesn't take a rocket scientist, therefore, to figure out that if the headmasters alone streamlined their administrative staff, they would be well on the way to kicking their dependency on deficit-spending and its twin brother, annual giving, in particular.

But convincing the typical headmaster that most of these "helpers" actually hinder more than help is probably wishful thinking. Realistically, short of a budget necessity or crisis similar to the one I inherited at Columbia Grammar way back when, "business as usual" will no doubt prevail, no matter how much money is being wasted unnecessarily on a bloated administration. Regrettably, the only known remedy for this unfortunate but common circumstance is board intervention—however unpleasant and awkward such intervention might initially appear. While boards are understandably reluctant to take such steps, "biting the bullet" only hurts momentarily. The results soon enough will make it all worthwhile.

THE PROOF IS IN THE PUDDING

Let's not generalize any further. Let's actually test this "golden rule" of private school management, that at *any private school where the endowment is as great as or greater than the operating budget, the amount of waste each year is equivalent at a minimum to the size of the annual fund*. Theory is one thing, facts are another. So come join me for a tour of The Other School, and we will see for ourselves whether there are any positions over there that can be eliminated without damage to the school's academic program or its ability to carry out its administrative responsibilities efficiently and successfully. While we can't actually take a real, live tour of The Other School, we can look at its rather typical administrative chart. Let's compare The Other School's actual administrative structure with Columbia Grammar's.

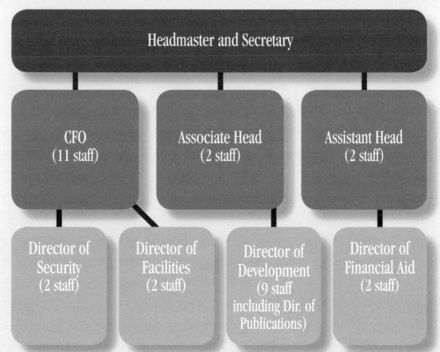

THE OTHER SCHOOL'S CENTRAL ADMINISTRATION

Headmaster and Secretary

CFO
(11 staff)

Associate Head
(2 staff)

Assistant Head
(2 staff)

Director of
Security
(2 staff)

Director of
Facilities
(2 staff)

Director of
Development
(9 staff
including Dir. of
Publications)

Director of
Financial Aid
(2 staff)

Here at The Other School they have a total of 32 staff positions including the headmaster and secretary. While this core administrative structure might seem reasonable to onlookers—and certainly it is not at all dissimilar to the core set-ups at most of the well-endowed K-12 private schools in New York City, regardless of size—the fact is that of these 32 positions, 22 do not exist at Columbia Grammar and Prep. In other words, our core administration, which carries out the very same sets of duties and responsibilities for an even *larger* number of students (30 percent more at Columbia Grammar), and an even *greater* number of faculty (35 percent more), and an even larger budget (25 percent more) is only one-third the size of The Other School's central administration alone.

Now, The Other School might well protest that it cannot get along without these 22 extra positions, that the school—but more so the headmaster himself—can't function effectively without two or three associate heads (each with his/her own secretary) or that the school needs seven or eight more people in the business office than we have at Columbia Grammar and so on. But far from having created a monster over here of over-worked staff who can't get their work done, Columbia Grammar and Prep School is actually well-run by well-paid and happy staff. No one who has ever taken a close look at us, such as New York State Association of Independent Schools (NYSAIS) visiting committees, other school administrators, parents needing to deal with the business office for one reason or another, and so on, has come away with anything other than a completely positive impression.

It may be counter-intuitive, but Columbia Grammar and Prep is no more difficult to "administer" today than it was 30 years ago, even though today we have over four times the number of faculty, three times the number of students, eight times the number of sports, three cafeterias instead of one, four gyms in place of one, two theaters instead of none, etc. We now have only marginally more administrators in our central administration than we did all those years ago.

The area of fundraising is no exception. The Development Office had three staff in 1981, raising less than $25,000 a year. Today, Development is only four people and has raised $6.4, $7.1, and $7.5 million respectively over these last three economically difficult years—$75 million cumulatively over my three decades, without the need of "extra" staff. Every layer and area of our administrative structure makes the same point over and over again: savings, on the one hand, and greater efficiency, on the other—and plenty of satisfied staff.

It should come as no surprise that the additional 22 positions over at The Other School come at a hefty cost. I can come up with a pretty good approximation based on both Columbia Grammar and Prep's payroll and published salary ranges provided by NYSAIS. Let's use a modest average salary of $95,000 per position plus 32 percent (our rate) for benefits such as medical, retirement, social security, long-term disability insurance, etc., and one comes to an average figure of approximately $125,000 per additional staff member, or approximately $2.75 million more in central administrative costs to manage the school at the top—over what Columbia Grammar spends for the exact same purposes. Though this is a conservative figure, it will serve our purposes here quite adequately.

Now, add to that figure an equally understated 15 percent for all the extra costs involved—heat, light and power, office space, cleaning, as well as paper, copy machines, cafeteria food, professional conferences, etc.— and you have another $412,000 for a grand total of (a very conservative) $3.162 million in additional expenses, and that's with just a glance at the top! This not only explains the bulk of The Other School's entire $4.2 million annual fund and where it goes, but more importantly, how and why it is totally wasted with not a single dollar helping a single student—or in any way remotely "offsetting tuition," or providing "greater financial aid," or "improving the quality" of The Other School's academic program. (And I'll bet that maintenance, housekeeping, and capital projects and purchases would account for the remaining $1 million in short order.)

But there is yet another amount, equally realistic though harder to quantify, that adds to the waste column. Waste always manages to remain largely hidden from view. Simply counting up the costs of needless positions can never in and of itself account for all of the waste occurring. Everyone thinks that when you add three positions to your staff that they can add up the cost of three salaries plus three benefit packages and calculate the additional administrative costs. It's not that simple. The additional staff increases waste exponentially. How? Because you have created a larger bureaucratic net, with more complicated meetings, more complicated interactions, more disagreements, all of which take more time and money to resolve and get things accomplished. When you reduce your staff to a minimum, you are not just getting rid of X number of positions, you're getting rid of all the interactions that contribute in a more subtle, but nevertheless equally real way to all this overall waste. So it's not just a matter of a arithmetic loss, but an exponential loss as well.

Consequently, much more money is actually being wasted over at The Other School than any simple tally of useless positions can demonstrate. If I could have an hour or two with The Other School's complete budget (WikiLeaks, where are you?), I could not only account for the entire $4.2 million represented by its annual fund, as we have already nearly done, but an additional amount represented by its average annual interest income from endowment, which admittedly is quite small these days. Nevertheless, whatever amount is represented realistically by endowment income can also be accounted for, though with a bit more detective work and analysis, and with the cooperation of The Other School to be identified clearly. We would have to unravel such hard-to-assess areas as "academic administration," a bit more sensitive and complicated to reduce than the strictly administrative, but equally unnecessary in some areas and wasteful in its own right, tech support and general expenditures on technology, deferred maintenance, cleaning and general upkeep, etc. Surely it can be done, though not as easily as central administrative expenditures, where large amounts of waste are always staring one in the face, so to speak.

The bottom line, however, is simply that the $4.2 million in annual giving and the much smaller amount in endowment income combined—a princely sum by anyone's standards—represent the total "waste" and "duplication" over at The Other School. The same sad state of affairs can be found at most of the other heavily endowed K-12 schools in New York City.

Yet despite this analysis, simple and straightforward as it is, you might still find it difficult to accept my conclusions, namely that all these millions of dollars are being squandered on nothing more valuable than administrative bloat. It just must seem to the uninitiated so utterly preposterous and unlikely that all these experienced and highly paid school heads, monitored as they are by trustees who by and large represent the business gurus of Wall Street, are actually running highly inefficient and wasteful bureaucracies. Indeed, it does seem unlikely and farfetched—but sadly, it is nevertheless the state of affairs at all the private schools that boast of high tuitions, large annual funds, and hefty endowments.

Well, to make matters even more confusing and even more difficult to accept, I will give you another counterintuitive thought to ponder. The Other School would have spent exactly the same amount of money on its academic program last year—and every year—even if no money whatsoever had been donated to the school in the first place. Donated money—as opposed to tuition—no matter how well-intentioned by the donor, does not end up either reducing tuition, or enhancing the academic program, or even increasing financial aid *if it is donated as part of the operating budget*, i.e. as part of an annual fund. This is why, in short, private schools, no matter how much money they raise in annual giving, are nevertheless barely able to maintain the status quo. No matter how much is raised in annual giving by a school, $4 million or twice that amount, the most that is accomplished by that school is to "balance" its budget.

And conversely, this is why Columbia Grammar and Prep has been able to move forward so rapidly and successfully over the past three decades—no voluntary giving goes to "balance" our budget. All of our voluntary giving, well over $20 million in the last three years alone, and nearly $75 million over the past 30 years, has gone into improvements—much better faculty salaries and benefits, new and improved buildings and facilities, lower student/faculty ratio and increased programs, both academic and extracurricular—and none into closing that suspicious, and unnecessary, "gap" between tuition and the so-called actual costs of education.

HOW RIGHT YOU ARE, PROFESSOR PARKINSON!

Overstaffing and waste, and its twin brother administrative inefficiency, seem to be universal to all institutions to one extent or another; from the tiny and cloistered world of private schools, where it is largely kept from public view; to government bureaucracies and big business, where waste is understandable, if not expected; to colleges and universities, where one would assume it could and should be avoided. Few, if any, administrative structures ever manage to escape altogether the almost inevitable tendency to develop a bloated bureaucracy and to waste an ever-larger proportion of otherwise precious resources. Bureaucracies seem inevitably to expand, and the waste thereby produced seems to grow accordingly, eventually leaving little rational connection between a particular administrative structure and the original purpose it was created to serve.

Why is this so, and more importantly, does it have to be this way?

It would seem, based on common sense, that bureaucracies need not inevitably become bloated or wasteful. Indeed, they rarely start out that way; they just become that way over time, gradually and *seemingly* inevitably. But the regrettable and undeniable reality is that virtually every bureaucracy, in the end, does in fact lose its way, becoming both wasteful and inefficient, which in turn suggests that the answer to the "why" question is a lot more complicated and puzzling than one might at first assume. And perhaps those of us who perversely enjoy fighting against the inevitable are simply "whistling in the dark." Maybe, just maybe, if I were to be brutally realistic with myself, bureaucratic bloat might even be right around the corner from Columbia Grammar's main entrance, simply biding its time to strike. Just maybe then, no matter what suggestions I might be offering here as an antidote, the problem of bureaucratic overspending is largely incurable.

Scholars on this subject have often enough come to such a conclusion. And in this regard, no one has explained the seemingly intractable nature of bureaucratic bloat—this counterintuitive relationship between the amount of work to be done and the number of staff required to do it—

better than the remarkable student of social behavior, C. Northcote Parkinson. A British naval historian, Parkinson combined a group of remarkably hilarious, but at the same time, deeply insightful essays into a small book entitled *Parkinson's Law* (1957). This masterful analysis of human behavior within bureaucratic institutions contains a number of "laws" that together reveal the follies and self-defeating ways of bureaucracies in the modern world, especially in business and government. *Parkinson's Law* certainly leaves the reader convinced that if it is not literally inevitable, then surely it is at least highly likely that *every* bureaucracy will at some point, usually sooner rather than later, develop "duplication," "waste," and "inefficiency." And schools, every bit as surely as governments and businesses, as all other organizations that grow large enough to count themselves bureaucracies, will become examples over time of Parkinson's "law," not to mention the butt of his considerable wit and humor.

The essence of Parkinson's insights into the nature of bureaucracy is wonderfully and succinctly expressed in his most fundamental law of all, which states: *Work expands so as to fill the time available for its completion.* Understanding this greatest of all insights into the nature of bureaucracy will help us to understand the puzzling disconnection between the number of people working in a given bureaucracy—even staid old private schools—and the work to be done.

Prior to going off to college and my discovery of *Parkinson's Law* as a freshman, I encountered Parkinson's wisdom first hand. I recall with great fondness and amusement my two summers as a high school student working for the road maintenance division of the City of Richmond, Virginia. We would be sent out to patch potholes in crews of six, though I cannot recall on even a single occasion when all six of us were working at the same time. Our standing joke was that it took one able-bodied man to patch a pothole and five to watch. Parkinson would have loved spending a day with us! If the City of Richmond in its great wisdom had paid any two of us twice the hourly rate of 65 cents an hour, we would have patched every pothole in the city with time to spare. As it was, about a half dozen crews of six each would dutifully go out each morning with little to show at the end of the day in terms of work accomplished (potholes patched).

Often, if not always in the long run, the amount and nature of the work to be done has a *decreasing* relationship with the *increasing* number of people hired to do it. As Parkinson himself put it: "The fact is that the number of the [administrators] and the quantity of the work are not related to each other at all. The rise in the total of those employed is governed by Parkinson's Law and would be much the same whether the volume of the work were to increase, diminish, or *even disappear*" (emphasis mine). One could cite countless instances of how positions within a bureaucracy get completely disconnected from the original purposes and goals they were designed to serve.

You need take only one isolated instance at our own little school to begin to appreciate the truth and importance of Parkinson's insights into how and why bureaucracies needlessly grow. Our Chief Financial Officer handles a budget of over $50 million these days, up from $1.1 million 30 years ago. You should keep in mind that our operating budget, based on statistics supplied by the New York State Association of Independent Schools and the Guild of Independent Schools, places us well within the top five among private schools, taking into account schools from all five boroughs. Our CFO also handles over $5.3 million in financial aid, up from $90,000; $10 million in endowment, up from zero; 195,000 square feet of floor space, up from 35,000; and the same progression could be pointed out in a dozen or more other areas under the CFO's responsibility. More work? Actually, not at all! And certainly not more work by virtue of the larger amount of money involved, which is the most common reason or excuse or rationalization or explanation given by other schools for increasing their business office staff. The fact is, more staff would actually create more work, not less. As Parkinson concludes, far from reducing work, *"Administrators make more work for each other—not less."*

Had our CFO taken the path that virtually every other private school has taken over this same period of years, especially those that have grown similarly in enrollment and physical plant, namely, to hire a new staff person every time the budget grew in some tangible or quantifiable sense, then surely today we would have a school bureaucracy that felt bloated and inefficient on the one hand, and full of staff who actually feel *overworked*, on the other. However, our CFO did not hire a Budget Director, or a Comptroller, or a Financial Aid Director, or a Facilities Coordinator, or an Assistant or Associate CFO—all of which you will find at many other private schools our size in New York City. And needless to add, he did not hire all the many "support staff" all these positions would naturally have "needed." Nor, I might add, did we need to find six or seven new offices for these staff, in place of using that valuable space for more important academic purposes. "And that," quoting Robert Frost, "has made all the difference."

Our Chief Financial Officer has yet to feel "overworked" or "stressed" (He would be the first to tell me if he were), and no school—bar none—runs as efficiently as Columbia Grammar and Prep. And the net result of all this for our school is that we never developed a so-called "gap" between tuition income and operating expenses that our unsuspecting but generous parents would have had to fill each and every year *ad infinitum*.

The difficulty of getting the modern manager—whether it's a college president, the head of a private school, or the CEO of a Fortune 500 company—to appreciate the fact that an institution's state of health has everything to do with the number (the fewer the better) and quality (fewer but each paid more) of its administrative staff was recognized years ago by Parkinson as well. As he so insightfully expressed it: "Every student of human institutions is familiar with the standard test by which the importance of the individual may be assessed. The number of doors to be passed, the number of his personal assistants, the number of his telephone receivers—these three figures, taken with the depth of his carpet in centimeters, have given us a simple formula that is reliable for most parts of the world. *It is less widely known that the same sort of measurement is applicable, but in reverse, to the institution itself*" (emphasis mine).

On the other hand, private school heads, most trustees, and unfortunately many parents mistakenly assess a school's health in terms of the greatest number and specificity of administrative positions, not to mention, as we have, the size of its endowment and annual fund. Walk into any private school that has all its administrative bases covered, so to speak, and you will find a school that is quite confident of its health and well being. I would venture to say further that the vast array of administrators with their intimidating titles and large and well-appointed offices, actually give parents a sense of assurance, even well-being, that the institution is in good hands and is ready to solve all problems, large and small.

However, in reality, nothing could be farther from the truth. As Parkinson points out, the *reverse* is actually the case. Such a school is in *a state of decline*. Wherever you find a school with a full contingent of administrators ready and able to carry out every conceivable type of administrative chore—from the smallest, such as making sure the copy machines are always loaded with paper, to ordering sufficient amounts of coffee for all the school's many pots, to the largest administrative chores, such as annual budget processes and five-year strategic plans—you surely know that such a school is headed for trouble. If not for the fact that large doses of annual giving and endowment income were masking the reality of bureaucratic bloat and inefficiency, the dangers facing such institutions would be immediately, or at least much more apparent than they are.

But even so, the underlying fact that a private school is going nowhere, or worse is actually in an state of decline, will become readily apparent at the first sign of real pressure: a shortfall in enrollment, or a decline in voluntary giving, or a reduction in endowment income. Private schools need to wake up now to the task of running more efficiently, without a reliance on deficits, annual giving, and the like. You would think that the "sub-prime mortgage" fiasco, the Bernie Madoff scandal, and the rapid demise of Bear Stearns and Lehman Brothers would have sounded enough of a warning bell to wake the average school headmaster "from his dogmatic slumber," as Immanuel Kant might have characterized it. My guess is that endowments will probably have to decline even further and annual giving will have to weaken even more to get the typical private school head or trustee to honestly question the standard practices of beginning each school year with an ever-larger gap in the operating budget.

Would it not make prudent sense to begin slimming down now on a voluntary basis? Indeed, isn't such an attitude at the very heart of what a headmaster's long-term responsibility should be in the first instance—and certainly at the core of a board's long-term fiduciary obligation? Moreover, the money saved could be put to immediate use in improving the school, and the headmaster of such a lucky school could at the same time get the practice and experience he/she will need to run the school efficiently when hard times come to stay. Then, when the day arrives, as surely it will, when out of necessity, a school must indeed operate efficiently, the head will actually be able to do so—and without losing a lot of sleep.

THE ETHICS OF ANNUAL GIVING
(OR, IS IT EVEN LEGAL?)

Let's now return to the moral and legal claims made by private schools for annual giving. Putting aside for the moment my view that annual giving does little more than sustain a school's administrative bloat, let's look more closely at the moral and legal claims schools make in defense of annual funds as essential parts of their operating budgets. Can annual giving stand up as worthwhile and practical on moral or ethical grounds alone, even if the many other claims for its goals are misleading at best?

First, the moral issue: If you recall, virtually all private schools claim that annual giving, by supplementing or offsetting the costs of tuition, promotes diversity by making private education more affordable to a wider range of families. In other words, that by giving low or at least lower income families a shot at a private education, annual giving has an ethical dimension and puts it on the "high road" of voluntary giving—at least, that is what the unsuspecting parent is supposed to believe.

However, as we have seen, annual funds do not in fact lower the cost of tuition. Nevertheless, for argument's sake, let's assume for the moment that they do, that in fact thanks to the generosity of parents who give to the annual fund, tuition is indeed lower than it would otherwise be. Does that make the situation ethical? Hardly. What in effect is happening is that all the families in a private school, not just those who need it, end up receiving the very same discount. So at any private school with a large annual fund you'll find that about three-quarters of the families are getting an automatic discount when they really don't need one at all!

If characterized in moral terms, I would call this situation unethical and not the opposite, as fundraising brochures would have you believe. You can hardly rationalize or justify this circumstance on ethical grounds, as schools try to do, by focusing solely on the fact that a quarter of the families in the school who legitimately do need financial assistance would in fact also benefit from lower tuition. From a strictly moral or ethical point of view, the fact that three quarters of the parent body is receiving an automatic discount that is not in any way remotely needed or deserved is much more troubling than the fact that a quarter of the lowest income families are theoretically being helped along with the rest. In actual fact, a school's financial aid program—not voluntary giving—is the appropriate and effective way to help all those families who cannot afford the cost of private school tuition. Only these families need their tuition costs offset or discounted.

Schools that bother to think about this issue sometimes try to justify this situation by claiming that the "wealthy" families who are getting this "automatic discount" make up for it by donating comparable or greater amounts of money to the annual fund on a voluntary basis—by closing the so-called "gap." The fact is, however, one has nothing to do with the other. If you want to help needy families, donate money for that purpose—to a scholarship fund. Lowering tuition for everyone not only doesn't actually serve to accomplish that goal, it creates a self-serving ethical problem as well.

Moreover, all of us who run private schools know quite well how many families each year who easily have the means to give to the annual fund either don't or give less than their so-called fair share. Somewhere in my distant past I recall reading that John Paul Getty prided himself on never giving a tip, other than that one instance early in his life when he gave a 10-cent tip to a taxi driver and regretted it ever after. It is pretty clear that in whatever school John Paul Getty placed his children, he did not give to the annual fund. While we don't have a lot of John Paul Gettys in our schools who are at the same time excessively rich and excessively stingy, we do have enough parents who get the automatic discount when not needed, leaving us with the uneasy conclusion that our annual giving programs are both wrong-headed and far from ethical.

If we turn now to the legal rationale for annual giving, we will get an even clearer idea of how and why annual giving has gotten sidetracked over the years from its original purpose of actually improving schools to its present state of affairs, which in effect is accomplishing nothing more than substituting an ever-increasing amount of pre-tax dollars for after-tax dollars. The primary purpose of annual giving today is simply to preserve and perpetuate the status quo—a cheaper way to operate a school—not, as it should be, a way to move the school forward. This has created not only an unethical situation out of annual giving but unfortunately an illegal one as well.

At first glance, annual giving appears to be a "legal" way to get financial support from the government (in reality, other taxpayers) by taking advantage of the tax-exempt status of private schools. In effect, according to private schools, the annual fund allows a donor to pay a portion of tuition, that is, to offset it with tax-deductible dollars in the form of a voluntary gift. In this way the parent or donor gets the government to subsidize his or her child's education—and every other child in that particular school as well—by virtue of the tax-deductibility of the gift. It's a win/win situation for both parent and school.

But if we extend this argument to its logical conclusion, if in other words a school's annual fund continued to grow into the future as it has in the past—becoming a greater and greater percentage of the operating budget—its annual fund would eventually constitute 100 percent of the operating budget. Under such circumstances, parents would be paying for their child's education completely in tax-deductible dollars. Clearly, this would be illegal and in direct violation of the IRS tax code governing gifts to tax-exempt organizations. You are strictly not allowed to pay for "goods and services" in tax-deductible dollars, not even in part, and certainly not in whole.

While it might appear far-fetched to think of an annual fund as representing the total operating budget of a private school, it is not at all farfetched to think of it as routinely encompassing 20 to 30 percent, or even 35 to 40 percent of the operating budget of some private schools. (Recent reports published by Princeton and Harvard revealed that endowment income alone covered 45 percent and 42 percent of their respective operating budgets. All that income came from taxpayer subsidized voluntary gifts. This is legal?)

The bottom line remains that from a conceptual point of view, annual funds—when used to pay for operating costs—are illegal, no matter what the size of the annual fund or percentage of the operating budget it replaces. Regardless of the variations from school to school, the "legal" issue remains unchanged: Annual giving, to the extent it offsets or replaces or in any way "pays for goods and services" (i.e. your child's education), constitutes a violation of the tax code.

Historically, the purpose of granting tax-exempt status to private schools was not to allow voluntary giving to substitute for tuition, but to pay for capital items over and above the annual operations of the school. Tuition, not voluntary giving, represents, legally and rightfully, payment by the parent for the goods and services provided to a student for his or her education. In effect, those goods and services are the "operating budget of the school." "Support for the basic operation of the school" should not be, contrary to what every school's annual fund brochure assures its parent body, "deductible for income tax purposes." Contrary to what every other private school claims, tuition and only tuition should go into its "checking account," to use one school's terminology, while all gifts, voluntary donations, etc., should go strictly into its "savings account." The former should be used for the operation of the school and the latter for growth and improvements—*checking for the present, savings for the future*.

This conclusion should come as no surprise to anyone. Neither should it come as a surprise to anyone if the IRS someday in the not-too-distant future, perhaps, puts its foot down and declares gifts to the annual fund illegal, at least those that "offset" tuition costs. After all, there is a relatively recent precedent in the private school world that should have come as a warning to us all. When I started headmastering in 1981, it was routine practice for Columbia Grammar and all other private schools to have auctions as the centerpiece of our spring benefits. We still do, as a matter of fact, but with a big difference. We no longer are allowed to give a successful bidder a receipt for the full price of whatever that person purchased through the auction. Rather, thanks to IRS insistence, we now subtract the market value of the auction item from the price paid—what remains, and only what remains, is tax-deductible by law.

So, for example, if someone is the successful bidder for two airline tickets to Paris, he or she may only declare as a tax-deductible gift to Columbia Grammar what remains after the market value of the tickets is deducted from the successful bid. Whoever donated the two tickets to Columbia Grammar already had received a tax deduction for the value of the tickets. Hence, to give the bidder another tax break for the same amount would, of course, be a duplication of a deduction already taken for that item. Likewise, and more to the point, giving a tax deduction to anyone for "goods and services" received—in this case, two tickets to Paris—is also illegal. Only what you voluntarily donate to a school with no expectation of goods or services in return can legally qualify as tax-deductible.

To take our analogy a step further and apply it to annual giving, the amount of the so-called "gap between tuition and the costs of educating a child" in a particular school should be deducted from every annual fund gift and only the remainder, if any, should qualify for a tax-deduction under IRS rules.

As I recall, it was about a dozen years ago, after many years of growing abuses by private schools and many other types of tax-exempt organizations through their fundraising auctions, that the IRS finally put a halt to this illegal but nevertheless routine practice. The only difference that I can see between the auction abuses and annual fund abuses is the fact that the former usually involves physical objects such as airline tickets, dinner at a fancy restaurant, and the like, while the latter involves "goods and services" that are much less tangible—though every bit as real—a child's education. Both practices directly use the tax-deductibility of gifts to private, tax-exempt schools as a vehicle for using pre-tax dollars to buy goods and services at a discount—auction items, in one instance and private education, in the other.

It was the excessive and growing use of auctions to fund private education that finally forced the IRS to step in. Similarly, in my view, it is the excessive and growing use of annual giving to "offset" or pay for an ever-growing proportion of tuition that will, once again, force the hand of the IRS. It should, as I said, come as no surprise when the IRS similarly declares annual giving off-limits as regards to qualifying as a tax-deductible gift, but rather money paid for "goods and services received." And schools with large endowments and ever-expanding annual funds will have no one else but themselves to blame. Remember: I am simply the messenger, not the culprit.

Of course, we can blame the IRS for getting private schools into this mess in the first place. One need only take a small logical step to figure out that this gap must have begun at whatever time the tax code was changed to allow not-for-profits to accept donations on a tax-deductible basis. At whatever point the federal/state government initiated the now universal 501(c)(3) statute governing not-for-profit schools, those very private schools and other similarly designated institutions started raising money in amounts and ways not possible before 501(c)(3).

This opportunity was recognized immediately by private schools, not to mention colleges and universities, of course, and so the ever-more-prominent history of annual giving began. Moreover, you would have to be quite a slow learner not to have recognized right away that here was a way to have some of your expenses covered with tax-deductible dollars. Now I am sure that the intent was a laudable one in the beginning. Alumni, friends, as well as parents, could donate money for libraries, gyms, endowments for programs and teachers, and better facilities of all types, that couldn't otherwise be funded through tuition dollars alone. These are all wonderful reasons to raise money through voluntary giving, and genuinely constitute "extras" that serve to move a school forward. All of these goals, and many other similar ones, go beyond the basics of the "operating budget" as such and fall therefore perfectly within the spirit and intent of 501(c)(3). These purposes were intended to be, and should always remain, the legal reasons underlying voluntary giving to tax-exempt schools.

Clearly, the realities of annual giving do not match up at all with the laudable claims that private schools typically make when soliciting their alumni and parents. Annual giving does not offset the costs of tuition; it doesn't provide the money needed to pay for all those "extras" that make a school special and improve its educational value; it can hardly be characterized as ethical; and, finally, it is marginally legal at best. As bad as all that might be, which taken together is more than enough reason to drop annual giving at the earliest possible moment, the most harmful reason of all is that *annual giving diverts the enormous value and potential of fundraising away from the critical task of improving a school to merely preserving the status quo.*

If a school with a large annual fund, for example, needs at the same time to carry out capital improvements—build a new building or plan major renovations, significantly improve faculty salaries far above usual increases, or double its financial aid budget—it must marshal enough strength, energy, and generosity to raise a significant amount of money over and above an already large annual fund effort. Some schools, especially in New York City, can do both, but most schools, even many in New York City, cannot. But even those schools that have the energy and wealth in their school communities to do both would be better off putting their annual fund dollars to much better use.

Every private school head should have the primary duty of examining the school's administrative structure on an ongoing basis to ensure that every dollar in voluntary giving goes toward the future—never the present. The only way to guarantee that this outcome will occur is for the board of trustees to insist, as a matter of policy, that the *total operations* of the school remain within the parameters set by tuition income. All voluntary giving, again as a matter of policy, in turn should go toward specific projects, goals that are clearly outside the operating budget and are just as clearly long-term and permanent in nature.

One thing is certain: If you keep dumping all that generosity and goodwill on the part of parents each year into the "unrestricted operations of the school," in effect the annual fund, then you will surely as anything have nothing to show for it in the end. What a pity for the parents and students of those schools that the generosity of the school community was spent on nothing more constructive than administrative duplication and overstaffing—a private school version of a "black hole."

THE ENDOWMENT TRAP

Most if not all readers will likely be somewhat puzzled by my view that "endowments" do as much harm to a school's budget as do "annual funds." Endowments, if they are big enough, have this almost unqualified reputation for solving virtually all of a school's financial problems. Private school heads—and even more so, college and university presidents—literally salivate at the thought of large and growing endowments. Endowments, after all, support programs, provide income for scholarships, create "permanent chairs," fund lecture series that otherwise could not be afforded, as well as countless other activities at every school and college that together create an intellectual and cultural world unto itself. And perhaps, best of all, endowments provide, as every endowment campaign emphasizes, "money for a rainy day," security against the unforeseen dangers lurking outside the ivy walls. As The Other School so aptly puts it, "Annual giving is for the checking account, while endowment funds are for the savings account."

Well, I am sorry to report, endowments unfortunately do not live up to their rosy reputation. In fact, endowments cause all sorts of financial problems and risks, in many respects more thorny and stubborn—certainly at the college and university levels—than annual funds create at the secondary school level for private schools. So, let's have a closer look at endowments to see why they might not be the solution to a school's financial needs that they are always advertised as solving.

First of all, what is an endowment? As far as private schools and colleges/universities are concerned, it is money given to an institution to provide income for a program or activity, such as Greek and Latin or music programs, a Chair of Women's Studies, a sports team, scholarships, and so forth. Just a few days ago, I received an annual fund publication from a prominent, well-endowed private school in New York City listing 142 named endowments in its back pages. So when it comes to a large and long-standing college or university, say Harvard or Yale, you will find literally hundreds upon hundreds of endowed programs and activities at any given time, stretching back many decades, if not centuries. Virtually all endowments carry an important legal stipulation, namely, that the institution to which the endowment money was given can never (except under dire circumstances) use the principal itself, but can only spend the interest earned from the principal in support of the "named and endowed activity or program." In other words, the capital, namely the original gift, must be preserved in its entirety—in perpetuity. This legal requirement, while perfectly reasonable from the point of view of the donor, is of the utmost importance in understanding the problems universally caused by these otherwise generous and welcome financial gifts to a school or college. Endowments are almost always restricted in nature, and it is that legal restriction in the final analysis that becomes a problem over time.

The basic problem with endowments is that the endowed principal rarely, if ever, provides sufficient income over the long run for the program or activity being funded. The bottom line is that you can't sustain a school's (or college/university's) programs—academic or sports or scholarships or a simple lecture series—through endowment income alone. Whether it is a rowing club or a Chair of Egyptian Studies, scholarships for Native Americans, or a chamber music series, the *operating expenses of the endowed activities over time always outpace the income from the original endowment*. When that point is inevitably reached, the "additional funds" needed to sustain the endowed programs must by necessity come out of the operating budget—hence an increase in the infamous "gap" we find in every school's annual budget.

While private schools rely less on endowments and more on annual giving each year to close their gaps, colleges do the very opposite. Colleges and universities rely very heavily on their hundreds of endowments, leading to enormous gaps in the operating budget, accumulating incessantly and inexorably over the years. This is why Harvard, Yale, and Princeton— with the three largest endowments in America and probably the entire world—have by far the largest gaps. I am always hearing people ask the question, with an incredulous look in their eyes, how and why Harvard could possibly run even a small deficit given its $36 billion in endowment at least in 2008? Well, the answer is somewhat counter-intuitive, as is much of what I have to say about school finances in general. Surprisingly, the answer is that they have too many, not too few, endowed programs. Simply put, endowed programs do not and cannot pay their way on the basis of endowment income alone. And unfortunately, tuition cannot close the gap either, because to do so would make costs prohibitive for at least half of the present student body.

One is left with few solutions to this universal dilemma. The solution that colleges and universities have typically chosen has proven to be a very risky and dangerous solution at best, as the last two years of the financial "recession" have so dramatically shown, to increase the percentage of "profit" or "income" from their endowments in order to make their programs sustainable. Hence, Harvard, Yale, and Princeton, just to name the most notorious and prominent of the heavily endowed colleges and universities, have resorted to investing in risky hedge funds; real estate deals; stock investments of all sizes, shapes, and categories—all in the name of greater yields. Would any sane and/or prudent college or university "speculate" with money that was given to it in good faith—for perpetuity—if it did not have to in order to pay for its promised and advertised programs? Of course not! Speculating in this way with essentially "sacred" endowment funds is irresponsible and basically immoral, certainly embarrassingly desperate.

But all the heavily endowed colleges and universities, and quite a few private schools in New York City, were caught red-handed when the market crashed four years ago. One private school admitted publicly that its considerable endowment had been largely invested in five different hedge funds, all of which crashed in the crisis, losing about 40 percent of the school's endowment within a few short months. These private schools and colleges behaved, and probably still behave, in this irresponsible way for the simple and sad reason that they can't pay their bills without resorting to the sort of risk-taking that itself led to the kind of financial catastrophe we are experiencing at this time. If the newspapers and magazines have it correctly analyzed, Harvard has lost 40 percent of its endowment over a two-year period—down to $19 billion from $36 billion. And to compound problems, the $19 billion is hardly yielding a pittance these days, certainly not enough to cover more than a small fraction of its previous yield during the heydays.

All this adds up to a growing "gap" on both the private school and college/university levels, followed understandably and predictably by a growing frenzy of fundraising by all schools. Unfortunately, parents and college alumni are becoming both reluctant and unable to continuously bail out their alma maters, and students can't be expected to bear the brunt of all these shortfalls by paying excessively higher tuitions. College students are in enough debt as it is without the expectation of picking up the tab for colleges and universities who have speculated with endowment funds. Parents, students, and alumni are rightfully expecting school heads and trustees to figure out a better and saner model for sustainability, one that relies more on living within the parameters of tuition and fees, and less on tax-deductable handouts and excessively high tuition increases.

I could give the reader countless examples at both the private school and college levels of programs whose present costs far exceed the income generated by the permanent endowment funds themselves, but it would simply belabor the point unnecessarily. The bottom line is that both annual funds and endowment funds, if not handled with the utmost care and attention to their potential risks and dangers, invariably lead to financial problems that show up first and foremost as a "gap" in the operating budget. And only by keeping a check on overspending and waste—the inevitable bureaucratic bloat that is strangling our well-endowed private schools and colleges—will the leadership of our schools finally be on the road to true "sustainability," freeing themselves of the "deficit" mentality, once and for all.

THE STATE LOTTERY AND
THE NEW YORK CITY PUBLIC SCHOOLS

The waste we see at private schools is not all that different from what you find in the public school system. To all those well-meaning folks who over the years actually bought lottery tickets to help improve public education—and, of course, get a chance to become rich themselves—I express a heartfelt apology on behalf of the state governments that falsely solicited your dollars with this otherwise laudable motive. Surely, you must remember all those enticing and clever slogans during the Koch/Dinkins/Giuliani eras (and now Bloomberg) such as, "Take a chance on a child's education," "Invest a dollar in a better future for New York City's children," and the like. Well, nothing of the sort ever happened, of course—and the question is: Why?

Yes, New Yorkers have invested their dollars over the years and the millions have become billions, but if anything has changed, it is that matters have gotten worse: higher student/faculty ratios, poorer scores, school buildings in greater disrepair, increased numbers of defections to private and religious schools by families who can afford the tuitions. The New York State Lottery alone has supposedly produced more than $10 billion for the public schools over the last couple of decades. Why hasn't all that money produced a noticeable improvement in the public school system? The answer, in a nutshell: *State lotteries are nothing more than large-scale annual funds for public education—with the very same counterproductive results!*

Lotteries, even with all their billions of so-called "extra dollars" for public schools, do no more good than annual funds do for their private school cohorts. A state lottery, like an annual fund in the private school world, does nothing more than pay for a portion of public education: It does not *add to or enhance* public education. *With or without a lottery, you would have the very same public school system—no better or worse, no richer or poorer.*

Just as we saw with annual funds, the proceeds from a lottery are co-mingled with the general school budget or, to use a technical term, are fungible. The only way that lottery proceeds will ever help the public school system (or annual funds will help private schools) is when administrative costs are strictly frozen as a pre-condition to "adding" lottery money to the public school budget—i.e. segregated from the operating budget. If you don't freeze administrative costs, no amount of so-called "extra" money will ever reach its intended purpose: teachers and students, which is to say, improve education. The "extra" money will simply end up substituting for items already in the operating budget—or worse, paying for more administrative staff. Administrative bloat is the first thing "extra" money is spent on by administrators, whether public school chancellors or private school heads. In brief, "extra" money from the New York State Lottery ends up doing for the public school system what annual funds do for private schools—more harm than good. The Lottery—at best—simply maintains the status quo; it does not provide for the better education so appealingly advertised.

There is perhaps no better illustration of what I am talking about here than the new position called the Chief Executive of Parent Engagement, that was created in 2010 by Joel Klein, the former Chancellor of the New York City Public Schools. While I admittedly know little more about the duties of this newly created position than Chancellor Klein's own description (as reported in *The New York Times*) of "ensuring a greater level of collaboration with parents and community groups that serve them," this new position nevertheless represents for me the quintessential example of bureaucratic bloat and duplication, not to mention needless waste of large sums of money. To begin with, what is a school principal's responsibility if not to "engage" his/her parent body and community groups within a school's purview? No one should be hired in the first place as a principal of a school who can't carry out such an essential and basic responsibility. You don't need a central office at enormous expense—assistants, secretaries, publications, large-scale meetings, etc.—to accomplish what already should be working at the appropriate level, namely, the principal's office itself, of each individual school.

A centralized office is not only going to waste millions of dollars of taxpayer (or lottery) money, but will take the initiative for "parent engagement" out of the hands of those clearly responsible and hopefully capable of creating it in the first place—the individual principals of each of the 1,700 or so public schools in New York City. The already top-heavy and bloated central bureaucracy of the public school system is the very last place one should turn to improve so-called "parent engagement" at the school level—the only place in fact it can be solved, if it is ever to be solved at all. It is certainly not through central bureaucrats with yet more "guidelines" and "manuals." "Chief Executive of Parent Engagement" might sound helpful on the surface, but unfortunately it is simply the latest example of what in fact we've seen these past 25 years or so with the oversized central bureaucracy of the public school system—and it's precisely where you will find all those proceeds from the New York State Lottery.

And if the position of "Chief Executive of Parent Engagement" isn't enough to convince you to storm the headquarters of the central bureaucracy, then one of former Chancellor Klein's last appointments while in office should strengthen your resolve. The well-meaning chancellor increased his immediate staff from three assistant chancellors to seven. When I read this, I had to rub my eyes in disbelief. Orwell must be turning over in his grave at the rationale given for this enormously expensive expansion of the central bureaucracy governing the public school system. According to a spokesperson for the chancellor, to quote one of our largest newspapers, "The moves—an effort that's meant, in part, to continue shifting central administrative functions towards the schools—will add a director of 'portfolio management' among other positions." If the chancellor's true intent is to "shift administrative functions towards the schools," then in my humble opinion he is doing the very opposite—and at enormous expense in dollars and energy. And this announcement comes to us in the context of the need to lay off many thousands of public school teachers because of a lack of funds. Orwell had a name for this sort of reasoning: Double Think. Perhaps it's high time that the mayor and the chancellor read *Parkinson's Law* and start applying its practical wisdom to our bloated city bureaucracy.

WHAT DOES YOUR HEAD COST?

While the waste in the public school system is deplorable and obviously large scale, one can still understand and even tolerate it to some extent, given the enormous task at hand. Keeping 1,700 schools and 1.1 million students safe, supplied, transported, and educated understandably requires a tremendous bureaucracy, and in spite of otherwise good intentions, that bureaucracy will, over time, become bloated and unwieldy. We might not like it as educators, parents, and taxpayers, but we can understand how it all came about—and even sympathize to some degree.

Private schools, however, have no such excuse. When waste, duplication, and inefficiency within the small and relatively easy-to-manage world of private education rears their ugly heads, they ought to strike a parent or trustee, even more so the school head, as unacceptable, certainly unnecessary. But boards of trustees seem almost oblivious to the existence of waste within their cloistered worlds of private schools. This has always puzzled me, because the solutions are staring boards right in the face so to speak, and resting right under their noses. Simply put, if boards of trustees of private schools are ever to determine whether schools are spending their administrative dollars wisely, they must stop asking the simplistic question, "How much is the head paid?" but ask the more relevant question, "How much does the head cost?" And an interesting way to understand how very different these two questions are—and how different are their implications—is to consider something called the Sarbanes-Oxley Act, which these days provides the legal framework for determining if a school or any not-for-profit is spending its tax-exempt dollars wisely—or not—at the top.

Although I have been arguing that the operating principle of the fewest number of staff being paid the highest possible salaries is one of the keys to efficiency as well as satisfaction in the workplace, our federal government seems to have other and more worthy goals in mind—just the opposite of my own perspective. In fact, nothing has represented for me a greater contrast to my own operating principles than the set of laws enacted on July 30, 2002, commonly referred to as Sarbanes-Oxley, after the two congressmen who sponsored the bill. Also known as the "Public Company Accounting Reform and Investor Protection Act," Sarbanes-Oxley aimed to restore public confidence in the nation's capital markets after the Enron, Tyco, and WorldCom scandals by setting new and enhanced standards for all U.S. public company boards, management, and public accounting firms.

Sarbanes-Oxley is admittedly a terrific *idea* and certainly constitutes a set of well-meaning goals. The problem, at least in the private school world, is that in spite of its noble intentions, it simply does not work to promote efficiency. Rather, it encourages the very opposite, leading to more people doing the same set of jobs less efficiently with more overall cost to the institution. Sarbanes-Oxley inevitably leads to more duplication of staff, not less, and certainly does nothing to create greater fairness or equity in the workplace which was its main objective in the first place. As my father was inclined to point out on every possible occasion, "The road to hell is paved with good intentions!"

Among other goals, Sarbanes-Oxley is intended to shed more light on the accounting practices of big business. I'm all for that. It was also designed to put some sanity and limits on executive compensation in light of the enormous pay packages of the CEOs throughout the larger business world. Good idea, as well! However, more often than not, when you try to "legislate" morality, even "common sense," it tends to backfire.

Let's look at one part of Sarbanes-Oxley—executive compensation—to determine if it helps us in our quest for more information, more fairness, and ultimately a better and more cost-effective system. While technically, Sarbanes-Oxley does not yet apply to the not-for-profit sector, the IRS has made it abundantly clear to all private schools that the "spirit" of these regulations will now be extended starting in the 2011-12 school year to cover our business practices as well, not just in the area of compensation, but how audits are conducted and reviewed by boards, how financial statements are reported to the public, and so on. But to take executive compensation as a case in point, the IRS is now requiring all not-for-profit private schools to keep the compensation of the top five highest earners within a range determined in large part by a survey of comparable schools. Hence, a private school in New York City, in order to comply with IRS notions of "fairness" in determining administrative salaries, must survey a "reasonable number of other private schools of similar size, mission, financial make-up, etc." In this way, a board of trustees, whose fiduciary responsibility it is to determine an "appropriate and fair compensation," will have an "objective framework" within which to reach these decisions.

Too bad it doesn't work that way.

Why? Because the more meaningful and important question to be asked is not what your headmaster or chief financial officer might make relative to his or her cohorts at comparable schools, but *what it costs at the top* to run a given school. Sarbanes-Oxley overlooks the fact that many schools, especially those heavily endowed ones with large annual funds, are spending enormously more money than they should for their top level staff to administer their schools—regardless of whether the headmaster (or chief financial officer) individually is highly paid or not. These extra expenditures add up to sizable amounts of money, altogether of a different magnitude than the relatively narrow and less consequential issue of the headmaster's compensation per se. Boards should of course be concerned with individual salaries, whether it's the headmaster's or some other highly paid administrator—but not at the expense of ignoring where the overwhelming bulk of waste and duplication is taking place throughout the administrative hierarchy of the typical private school.

Just one example from Columbia Grammar can illustrate this point in a glaring manner. Our Chief Financial Officer, as we've pointed out, wears a half-dozen or so key hats within our administration, from supervising and directing the entire business operations of the school to handling financial aid, overseeing security and maintenance, technology and all capital projects, as well as serving as second in command whenever I am away from the school. On the other hand, at other schools, separate individuals wear many of these very same hats—at great additional cost. To compare our CFO's salary with CFOs at other schools would be inherently unfair to him, and, more to the point, to require our school to pay him within this range, as Sarbanes-Oxley would have it, would create an obvious inequity. In brief, it would directly undercut our management goal of paying as few people as possible the most amount of money to do the greatest amount of work. Sarbanes-Oxley will end up making our world quite flat and homogenous, ultimately giving bloated bureaucracies a stamp of governmental approval—the opposite of what schools, indeed all not-for-profits, need.

But if you would like another example, one even closer and dearer to my own heart, here at a glance is my own situation: I preside over a pre-K-12 school of approximately 1,300 students, the largest in Manhattan. If you take the five largest private schools in enrollment (I would even venture to say the 10 largest), you will not find another school without at least one associate head and often two, occasionally three or four! The fact that I operate the school alone at the top with only one assistant/secretary is of no relevance to Sarbanes-Oxley. Sarbanes-Oxley could care less that one of our peer schools is spending on the order of 300 percent more to operate the school at the top. Nevertheless, if my salary is not within 10 percent of the average top five salaries of heads at peer schools, a penalty looms over the school's board, despite the fact that this situation has actually saved the school a minor fortune over the years. The matter is important to me not because I am underpaid, which I am not, but rather because this shortsightedness could lead to perhaps the single largest amount of waste and duplication in any private school.

The bottom line is that a school's trustees should compare, not head compensation from one school to the next, but the *overall cost of running its school administratively* with comparable schools—particularly with Columbia Grammar's administrative structure! By doing so, they would finally gather the information they need to fulfill their basic fiduciary responsibilities, namely, to answer the question whether the school is spending its tax-deductible dollars wisely or not. Sarbanes-Oxley is simply focused on the tip of the administrative iceberg. In actual fact, however, the fiduciary health of a school lies, as with most dangers, well below the surface.

THE FEDERAL GOVERNMENT AS ROLE MODEL

The mindset of overspending when there is no consequence, or at least no immediate consequence, is not, of course, the sole domain of schools, private or public. The most prominent example of this sort of behavior, as we know all too well, is our own federal government. Indeed, the federal government–actually just about every government from city to state on up to the highest levels of federal government–loves "deficit spending" every bit as much as private schools do. And the larger the city or state, the more in love with debt, and therefore deficit spending, a city or state will become.

Not surprisingly, "deficits" play essentially the same role in city, state, and federal budgets that "annual funds" play in private school budgets. With only superficial differences, annual funds have the same negative effects that deficits have on governments on all levels: each leads equally to over-spending and waste, and each puts the enterprise in question, a school on the one hand and a government on the other, in hock to the future. Annual funds, just like our federal deficits, pass on the liability largely to future generations, with almost casual indifference, I might add. Moreover, to carry the analogy a step further, both annual funds and government deficits continue to grow, accumulating debt upon debt until one day–in the future, of course–these unacceptable debt loads can no longer be sustained.

But the most interesting and indeed puzzling aspect of this analogy is that both schools and governments borrow money in direct proportion to how *little* each needs to borrow in the first place. America, for example, arguably the richest and best-endowed nation on earth, borrows the *most*–and at the *fastest rate*. The sale of treasuries, long-term bonds, ever-expanding trade deficits, borrowing from our own social security reserves to maintain our yearly operating budgets, and so on, altogether represent deficit spending at record levels. The federal government, in my humble view, ought not to be placing this growing debt on the shoulders of future generations, especially since this cumulative debt does little more than maintain the status quo—and nothing for growth and renewal. However, the more puzzling aspect of our government's propensity to borrow its way to "solvency" is the fact that the federal government *need not* create this debt in the first place. We seem to borrow for no better reason than that the money is made available to us—because it is easier and more convenient and takes less effort to borrow than to consider other alternatives. The fact is, as the richest and best-endowed nation in the history of the world, we have lots of alternatives to the seemingly unchecked borrowing we regularly pursue to pay our daily bills. And not surprisingly, this parallels the behavior of our richest private schools, where those with the largest endowments, the highest tuitions, and the best facilities—in other words, those with the least need to borrow in the first place—actually borrow the most and at the fastest rates possible.

There is irony in the fact that private schools have so much in common with the way the federal government operates. Each begins the fiscal year with a significant deficit, and each assumes that this way of operating is both normal and without adverse consequences. However, neither has any clear notion as to how much better off each would be if only it were to operate within the constraints of its respective income: tax revenues in the case of the federal government and tuition in the case of private schools. But, just keep in mind:

Annual giving is in reality equivalent to long-term debt, simply two sides of the same coin. Increasing the annual fund—something every private school does routinely—is the same therefore as increasing a school's long-term debt, with the dubious distinction of having nothing to show for it the following year!

The very same can be said of federal borrowing by selling ever-larger amounts of treasuries with the similarly dubious distinction of having nothing to show for it the following year!

Let's carry the analogy with the federal government a step further, beyond the obvious irony, to matters of greater substance. Hardly a day passes during these troubled economic times without mention of the federal government's growing deficit—in newspapers, magazines and websites, on talk shows, and incessantly during the campaign seasons. The most common guesstimate as to how much the government owes at the moment is around $15 trillion. Somewhere I read that our government has borrowed this staggering sum largely during the past 25 years alone. Now, let's suppose, for the sake of this intellectual exercise, that over this 25-year period the federal government had at the same time lived within the constraints of tax revenues, in other words did not use this "borrowed" $15 trillion dollars for its operating budget, but for *capital purposes* only: new roads, railways and high-speed locomotives, bridges, public universities, modern power plants, medical centers of all types, clean water, dams, improved levees for New Orleans, a new and reliable "grid" to carry electric power throughout America, and countless other capital projects.

The infrastructure of America would now be by far the best in the world. While we would owe today the *same $15 trillion dollars in debt* that we actually do owe, our competitive place would nevertheless be assured for the next century, and all of our bondholders (U.S taxpayers and the Chinese, Japanese, and Saudi Arabian governments) would be assured that these bonds, T-bills or whatever, would and could easily be paid off in the future. We would, in effect, have the wherewithal *to meet our financial obligations* with room to spare. The important point here is simple: *Debt is not the problem; the real problem is when you don't have anything to show for it.* In this regard, the federal government and private schools unfortunately have a lot in common. Federal debt and annual funds share one self-defeating trait: each plugs a hole in an operating budget. Or, to put the matter in negative terms, neither builds toward the future, which, outside of an emergency, is the only legitimate purpose for debt in the first place.

Now compare on the one hand, the federal government's approach to ever-increasing debt and the typical private school's approach to ever-increasing annual giving with Columbia Grammar and Prep's operating principles over the past 25 years on the other. Rather than borrow in order to *operate* our school, we have lived within the constraints of tuition, and at the same time have put all of our "borrowed" money—nearly $75 million in voluntary giving—into our future. While today we don't have one of those large endowments that many private schools in New York City are so enamoured of, more importantly we do have an infrastructure—new buildings, labs, wonderful families and students, one of the lowest student/faculty ratios to be found anywhere, a first-rate and highly paid faculty, a large and growing admissions pool, along with a solidified reputation for excellence—and this guarantees our bond holders and parents that they have the safest investment in town. And as we have painfully seen during this latest downturn in the economy, where endowments have stopped earning the big bucks—or any bucks at all—our infrastructure is indeed a much more reliable and permanent hedge against that inevitable "rainy day" than any endowment could ever be.

It basically doesn't matter how much you borrow or how much you fundraise, which together serve the same purpose, as long as both the borrowing and the fundraising are applied to a school's future as opposed to its operating budget. If we owed $100 million, or even more, we would still be in an enviable position because our "owed" money would represent the strength of our future, not a temporary support for the present. Once applied to a school's future, fundraising income and/or borrowed funds become an asset, a long-term benefit and in effect the best possible guarantee of future success and well being, both financial and otherwise. Conversely, if fundraising goes primarily or exclusively into the annual fund, into closing the "gap" in the operating budget, then all those well-meaning and generous gifts, regardless of how helpful they might seem on a short-term basis, become a liability and a sure sign of trouble in the future.

Private schools, just as our governments at all levels, have simply become too comfortable and too dependent on debt to operate and manage themselves financially. While the preferred form of debt among private schools goes by the euphemism of "voluntary giving," it nevertheless renders all private schools every bit as dependent on donations and gifts as the government is on such gimmickry and maneuvers—borrowing from Peter to pay Paul and in the last resort simply printing more money when the government needs it. Both forms of borrowing—government and private school—create a dependency on others for financial well-being and solvency, and both in turn inevitably lead to the loss of independence, the very attribute that private schools treasure and wish to protect the most. And just as with the federal government, private schools end up putting their futures in hock, supposedly and ironically on behalf of their constituents—students and faculty—the very ones ultimately who will suffer the long-term consequences of a future "gap" that can't be closed. The solution is as simple as living within—not beyond—one's means, namely, on tuition and tuition alone.

THE BEST KEPT SECRET IN TOWN

Most readers, especially those with a logical bent, will already have assumed that to make up for our lack of an annual fund, Columbia Grammar must simply be charging more than other schools in tuition. How else, after all, would we have been able to balance our own budget all these years without the help of an annual fund if not by charging more in tuition? Where else could all that money needed to fill our own "gap" have come from if not from voluntary giving and/or endowment income? The fact is, however—and this makes the question of our success even more interesting and puzzling—that we have consistently charged *less* on average, not more, than our cohorts at other private schools in New York City. Indeed, our original goal was not only to live on tuition alone, but to do so expressly without having to charge more than other schools.

As a struggling school with over-crowded and inadequate facilities in the early 1980s, an underpaid and understaffed faculty, and a rapidly declining reputation, Columbia Grammar could not have charged more than other schools because, as you might have guessed, this would have merely exacerbated what seemed like an already hopeless situation. Consequently, we made certain each year that we were charging less on average than our cohorts if for no other reason than to allow us to survive in what was then very much a buyer's market. In fact, as those living in New York City in those days will recall, at least a half dozen private schools—some quite long-standing and reputable—either closed their doors forever or merged with others in order to survive. Some of the best-known casualties included Walden, New Lincoln, McBurney, Baldwin, Rhodes, and Fleming, all of which closed, while Birch Wathen and Lenox had to merge in order to stay solvent. So to avoid the same fate, we made certain each year that we were charging less than virtually all of the other private schools—at least, all of the other K-12 schools.

Consequently, to make absolutely certain we knew where we stood in the galaxy of New York City private schools, we started conducting a yearly survey and have continued doing so for more than 25 years, comparing tuitions at K-12 schools within the five boroughs of New York City. Our statistical studies have always taken into account exactly what it would cost a parent to send a child to any one of the other 16 most prominent and competitive private schools in New York City starting at kindergarten on through to the high school years. Columbia Grammar and Prep can consistently be found in the middle to low end of this list, with the top being the most expensive, often $2,000 to $3,000 more per student. This has been true, and remains true today, whether we are compared at the lower, middle, or upper school levels, or whether we are compared with larger or smaller schools, more heavily endowed or less, co-ed or single sex, with large annual funds or not. Any way you compare our tuition and fees with those of other K-12 private schools in New York City—every mandatory cost included—you will readily see that in fact we have consistently charged less than most—but certainly always in the mid-range—in tuition than our counterparts, as you can see in the following chart:

TUITION & FEES COMPARISON 2010-2011

	GRADES K-4	TUITION & FEES	ANNUAL INCREASE
1	School A	$36,500	6.1 percent
2	School B	$36,250	5.0 percent
3	School C	$35,980	3.7 percent
4	School D	$35,915	6.7 percent
5	School E	$35,700	6.9 percent
6	School F	$35,670	4.8 percent
7	School G	$35,666	8.0 percent
8	School H	$35,600	7.2 percent
9	School I	$35,550	5.4 percent
10	School J	$35,434	5.3 percent
11	School K	$35,300	3.5 percent
12	School L	$35,200	3.5 percent
13	**CGPS**	**$35,123**	**4.4 percent**
14	School M	$35,025	4.7 percent
15	School N	$34,735	3.4 percent
16	School O	$33,500	4.9 percent

TUITION & FEES COMPARISON 2010-2011

	GRADES 5-8	TUITION & FEES	ANNUAL INCREASE
1	School A	$38,225	5.4 percent
2	School F	$37,202	4.6 percent
3	School C	$36,450	4.0 percent
4	School D	$36,428	5.3 percent
5	School B	$36,225	5.0 percent
6	School H	$36,150	6.6 percent
7	School G	$35,950	5.9 percent
8	School J	$35,889	4.9 percent
9	School E	$35,700	6.9 percent
10	**CGPS**	**$35,640**	**4.4 percent**
11	School L	$35,550	3.5 percent
12	School I	$35,550	3.5 percent
13	School K	$35,300	3.5 percent
14	School M	$35,025	4.7 percent
15	School O	$34,750	5.2 percent
16	School N	$34,435	2.9 percent
	GRADES 9-12	TUITION & FEES	ANNUAL INCREASE
1	School A	$38,800	5.1 percent
2	School F	$37,740	4.5 percent
3	School G	$36,950	6.9 percent
4	School D	$36,915	5.3 percent
5	School C	$36,500	3.7 percent
6	School H	$36,400	6.7 percent
7	**CGPS**	**$36,340**	**4.4 percent**
8	School J	$36,286	5.0 percent
9	School B	$36,225	5.0 percent
10	School M	$36,120	4.3 percent
11	School E	$35,700	6.9 percent
12	School L	$35,550	3.5 percent
13	School I	$35,550	3.5 percent
14	School K	$35,300	3.5 percent
15	School N	$34,962	2.8 percent
16	School O	$34,875	4.5 percent

Please make note of a common misunderstanding regarding comparable tuition costs among private schools in New York City: We have a one-fee total cost approach. In other words, our costs at each grade level encompass tuition and all fees. Other private schools, including those listed on the chart, charge separately for tuition on the one hand and fees on the other. When *The New York Times* or other publications call private schools to find out what they charge at a given grade, private schools typically respond by quoting tuition costs alone—and conveniently leave out the fees. Since we have one fee, we end up being placed—mistakenly—at the top of the chart, as in the January 26, 2012 *New York Times* survey. The truth, however, is that we are, as the chart above indicates, at the midpoint of costs when tuition and *all* fees are included.

In any case, the reader can with complete assurance put to rest the most obvious answer to our initial question as to how we get by—and get by so successfully—on tuition alone: The answer is emphatically *not* because we charge more in tuition. The answer lies elsewhere, and has everything to do with how we operate and manage our school.

So how do we provide students and faculty as much and most often more of everything that goes into the highest quality education all within the parameters of tuition alone and at the same time keep tuition at or below the mid-point of other K-12 schools in New York City? In other words, how do we manage to accomplish both efficiency and cost containment on the one hand, and satisfied faculty and staff on the other? Here is a little operating secret that has guided my hand over the years: *Hire the fewest number of administrators possible, and pay them each as much as possible.* Or, to put this principle in more practical terms, keep far fewer people on staff than you would find at comparable schools, but pay them much more than they would make at those other schools.

This is a very easy principle to apply in practice. Pick a half-dozen or so schools in your general area that are comparable to yours in size, mission, and budget. For each school, outline its administrative structure, count the number of staff, in the business and development offices, the number of maintenance staff and so on. Then devise a plan to operate with as few as one-half the staff you find at your counterpart schools. The object of this exercise, then, or the rule of thumb to be followed, is to run your school with half that number, while paying each of your staff a minimum of at least 25 percent more than their counterparts at those other schools. In this simple and straightforward way, you will run more efficiently with a happier staff, guaranteed.

Before applying your cost-cutting ax, however, let's make sure you understand the spirit, as well as the substance, of the approach I am recommending. This approach need not, and indeed should not be, applied overnight, at the cost of firing or otherwise letting loyal staff members go. On the contrary, our operating principle can and should in all cases be applied sanely and humanely *over time*. Retirements, departures, reassignments, and reorganizations, and early retirement all create sensible opportunities to reduce staff and make your administrative structure more efficient. And best of all, they free up funds to increase everyone else's salary.

Hence, of the six key administrative positions, excluding Headmaster, that NYSAIS keeps annual track of and publishes in the form of statistics statewide each year—Chief Financial Officer, Director of Admissions, Director of High School, Director of Maintenance or the Physical Plant, Director of Development, and Director of Lower School—*five out of the six highest paid independent school employees in New York State are employed at Columbia Grammar*. If this fact were made public with no explanation, most people would naturally and therefore *mistakenly* conclude that CGPS was spending too much money on managing the school. But, in fact, *the very opposite is true*. We spend less—a lot less—not more than other schools on administrative and management costs. And that is why, though it hardly needs repeating at this point, we can operate our school on tuition alone; we simply don't waste money on needless administrative positions. And indeed, it is why we can keep our tuition costs below the majority of our peer schools in New York City. In brief, *as few staff as possible paid as much as possible* is a formula that produces efficiency, a reduction of costs, and happy workers—the essential ingredients of any successful school.

THINKING INSIDE—AND OUTSIDE—THE BOX

Private schools, perhaps because they have such long and stodgy histories or perhaps due largely to the unusual level of success they have enjoyed in recent years, think and behave in very conservative and predictable ways—"in the box" so to speak. Too few heads of school are inclined, much less willing, to think "outside the box." Attitudes and philosophies about private school management are handed down from one head to another and accepted as gospel, even if these approaches end up costing our schools more than they should or even when policies violate common sense, as in the propensity and willingness of all private schools to begin each year with a deficit, even a very large one.

What particularly puzzles me, however, is the fact that the general issue of how best to manage a private school, and very specifically the question of why "deficit spending" itself is basically off-limits when it comes to dialogue and discussion among heads of school. Even if starting each school year with a deficit were indeed the best way to manage and finance a private school, the issue is nevertheless still worthy of discussion. But I have yet to see this question, so obviously worthy of thorough examination, even once placed on the agenda of a major conference of school heads during my over 30 years of running a private school.

I am sure that this subject is not ignored out of malice or any conscious attempt to avoid a potentially negative discussion. Rather, the silence is more likely the result of custom and routine at work. These are powerful forces, and the inclination to accept what seems to work well enough is an understandable one. "If it's not broke, don't fix it" applies to more than machines, and I suppose it applies in this instance to private school management. Nevertheless, private schools, however successful they might appear to be today, are far from perfect, and some objective self-examination of "business as usual" would do us all some good—before the day comes, when it surely will, when all schools are forced "involuntarily" to take a hard and objective look at themselves.

Fortunately there is an alternative. To all those private school heads who truly believe they can't get by without an ever-larger infusion of annual fund dollars—in other words, without an ever-larger "overdraft checking account"—and similarly to all those university presidents who feel they can't get by without ever-larger endowments, I suggest as required reading a relatively ignored but wonderfully insightful article detailing the effectiveness and success of small liberal arts colleges that at the same time operate on modest tuitions and negligible endowment income. In the *Chronicle of Higher Education* for June 2006, Richard Ekman, President of the Council of Independent Colleges, states:

"We may sometimes lose sight of the fact that a college's purpose is not to acquire wealth but to educate students. It's what small private colleges do best, by operating with a focus and efficiency that make the most of even fairly small endowments. Small, private colleges that face the combined pressures of small endowments and modest tuition revenue do better than public colleges by virtually every measure of institutional effectiveness and student success."

How do these small colleges without big bank accounts accomplish this success? You would think that these small colleges without endowments to speak of, negligible annual funds, and without public subsidies of any kind, large or small, would all be disappearing into oblivion—or at a minimum, shortchanging their students in countless ways. However, the "educational outcomes" point to the very opposite conclusions, as the statistics indicate. Instructional spending at these colleges has increased—not decreased—on average over 12 percent per capita, while their already modest endowments have actually decreased by 4 percent during the same period. Even under these worst-case circumstances, private colleges on average spend approximately twice the amount of money on each student's actual education as do public institutions. How then, do they provide students with smaller classes, more interaction with full-time professors, better counseling—in short, with a "more expensive" education than their publicly supported counterparts? "Out of necessity," as Ekman points out, the small, liberal arts college must "actively seek ways to control costs, while enhancing services. Income from a large endowment can enhance educational quality, but it is not the only means." And Ekman's concluding words are particularly worth remembering: "The most important way to measure the effectiveness of a college is by what it does for students, not by what it keeps in the bank."

Why, then, aren't private K-12 schools operating in the same fashion? Why, if it is so clearly beneficial and cost-effective to hold down "non-academic" expenses in order to provide more money for "academic" expenses, aren't all private schools behaving that way as a matter of common practice? And more to the point, why aren't the school's trustees, responsible as they are for the school's long-term financial help, keeping closer tabs on how a school spends, and misspends, its money? The answer is simply that, while it's true that trustees want to know how the money is spent, they are never quite in a position to figure that out, even though they get audit reports and they meet with the president of the university or private school four to six times a year—or more! When I was Vice President of Academic Affairs at the State University at New Paltz, I was in charge of the budget for the entire university. I knew where every penny went. But I can assure you that not a single trustee had any realistic notion of how we were spending money, no matter how hard and clearly we tried to present it.

But if you've never managed a school and you are a trustee, you never really get a sufficiently clear understanding of how the school operates and spends its money, much less why it spends its money. If you are a trustee, you are really dependent on the good judgment, managerial skills, know-how, and the integrity of the chief executive, the college president, the dean of a college, or the headmaster of a private school. But trustees, in order to carry out their fiduciary responsibilities properly, need to understand how it all works. The same goes for every administrative person in a private school, every headmaster, every associate headmaster, every college dean, every director of a school division. And, as I hope this book makes clear, all of us responsible for the proper management of our schools, from the lowest administrator to the highest ranking trustee, need to understand that there is a viable alternative to doing business as usual—an alternative to simply adding more administrative staff, and therefore raising more money, as a way of managing our schools successfully.

Many of our private schools today—even some of the most heavily endowed—are facing serious financial pressures, no different from those found throughout the world. Capital projects such as new buildings, better medical and retirement benefits, improved salaries, and countless other improvements and initiatives are being curtailed or postponed for financial reasons. What I hope this book does is give schools a way to reorganize, to free up money to accomplish the goals that otherwise cannot be afforded in today's economic climate. And to recognize at the same time that the only reason schools could accomplish them so readily in the past was that voluntary giving was free flowing and ever increasing. Heretofore, there was really little need to worry about how to control expenses, or how to manage a school. There was always that extra donor out there who would give you that extra gift, and the margin of error in how you were operating your school was something you simply didn't have to think about. Today, however, those of us who are responsible for running private schools have to think first and foremost about how to manage a school financially. Thinking exclusively or primarily about "academic excellence" and the so-called "higher virtues" is a luxury of the past. Our schools are businesses as well—and fragile ones at best—that need the most thoughtful care possible about finances and administration at the top.

"The Conclusion" that follows outlines in the simplest way possible the principles that guided us through our own three decades of growth and renewal as a school, as we faced similar financial pressures along the way, not to mention countless other problems. And we hope these principles, hard-earned as they were, provide other school heads today with a broad roadmap to creating better-run and more successful schools—and a way to avoid some of the financial problems that nearly ended Columbia Grammar and Prep's history as one of America's most reputable and long-standing private schools.

PART 3:

THE ROADMAP
TO OUR SUCCESS

*"I learned not to be too confident in any belief to which
I had been persuaded merely by example or custom;
and thus little by little, I delivered myself from many
errors powerful enough to darken the natural light and
incapacitate me from listening to reason."*

—Descartes from *Discourse on Method*

THE TWELVE PRINCIPLES

I n the course of writing of this book, I discovered that I had been operating all these years less on a carefully thought out "management philosophy" than on a propensity to rely on *instinct* and good old-fashioned *common sense*. However successful I might have been over the years, instinct and common sense are not exactly the professional attributes needed to serve as a blueprint for how to run a private school. But in the hope that my experience will be of some value to other school administrators today and in the future—and by analogy to bureaucrats everywhere—I would like to summarize my management philosophy into a number of key principles that have guided me over my 30+ years as headmaster:

PRINCIPLE #1: Don't assume something is being done right simply because it has always been done that way.

This first principle might strike the reader as somewhat trivial, or at least something that should be obvious to any person who finds him or herself thrust in a position of responsibility. In fact, however, it is a principle that virtually everyone, regardless of status, ignores. After all, it was Socrates, as Plato reminds us on many an occasion, who was judged by the Delphic Oracle to be the wisest among all men for the very reason that he, more than any other man, truly knew that he did not know. Suspending one's belief, questioning the status quo, thinking outside the box are all simply different ways of expressing a Socratic challenge to our natural tendency towards complacency and the acceptance of conventional beliefs. Descartes espouses the same principle in his famous *Meditations* when he makes the ironical claim that the essential first step to knowledge is the suspension of belief itself, a strict adherence to systematic doubt as the first and essential step to clearing the mind of old habits and beliefs.

And indeed, it was my willingness during that first week as headmaster to question one of the pillars of private school management and finances—the universal and long-standing belief held and followed by every head of school in America—that running ever-larger operating deficits and "closing" them with ever-larger annual fund campaigns—was the only correct, or at least the best, way to operate and manage a private school. I doubted the wisdom of operating a school in that fashion, and that doubt has served me and Columbia Grammar and Prep School quite well over the years. On the other hand, had we followed conventional wisdom back in 1981, perhaps we would have survived insolvency, but I seriously doubt that the school could have grown and prospered the way it has. Conventional wisdom, which is doing things the way they have always been done, has its place in life, to be sure, but that place is not in schools. Conventional wisdom is designed to keep things as they are, not to move things forward, but our schools, the very institutions that prepare our children for the future, need more than any other institutions in society to evolve and change constantly. Otherwise, we face the real danger of having children finish their schooling insufficiently prepared for the always surprising challenges of contemporary life. In brief, my advice to new heads of school: From day one, doubt everything, from how English and math are taught to how best to manage and finance a private school. This refreshing mindset will help you clear the path from old to new, and give you the best chance possible to run your school in an innovative and successful fashion.

PRINCIPLE #2: The administration of any private school primarily expands according to the amount of voluntary giving available.

This is the private school/college/university corollary of Parkinson's famous law: *Work expands to fill the time available for its completion*. With only the slightest adjustment, Parkinson's great insight can be applied to school bureaucracies, indeed, any bureaucracy, since they all follow the same tendency towards bloat and duplication. The slight difference that applies to private schools has simply to do with the source of the funding for the expansion of the administrative bureaucracy: *As fundraising goes up, the bureaucracy expands*. For government, the bureaucracy grows as tax revenues grow; for business, the bureaucracy grows as profits grow, and so on and so forth.

The point here is simply that schools, like government and business, respond bureaucratically to increased income by expanding accordingly. Schools receive income from three sources: tuition, endowment, and voluntary gifts. Therefore, it is easy to plot any school's (or college's) growth in administrative bureaucracy by simply doing a graph of its revenue growth. It is an easy and simple exercise. All you need are, say, the last 10 years of audits, which every school keeps on file. You will readily see that the growth in administration always equals or exceeds the growth in revenue, making it certain that the school at best can only maintain the status quo, since nothing is ever left over for *growth*. If you look at our chart going back 10 years (see page 206), you will see that our administrative costs increased far less than our academic costs and faculty salaries—hence our enormous surplus of funds to build new buildings and raise salaries to the highest tier among private schools in New York City. Simply put, the rate of expansion of the academic areas should always grow substantially faster than the rate of expansion in the administrative areas. If these two lines on your 10-year graph are growing farther apart as the years go by, then that more than any other numerical indicator constitutes proof positive that your school is in good financial health and that money is being spent wisely.

PRINCIPLE #3: Annual fund goals are never determined by the amount of need, but always by the amount of wealth in the community being solicited.

Have you ever wondered how schools come up with annual fund goals in the first place? Take The Other School, as an example. The Other School was seeking $4.2 million for the 2010-2011 year. Now, as a parent, or indeed any rational person, you would think that the $4.2 million represents all the children in The Other School multiplied by the amount The Other School claims is the "gap" between tuition and the "actual cost of educating a child in The Other School for the 2010-2011 school year." That's what their fundraising brochure claims, and it is what you would naturally assume. Math never fibs, or does it? Well, if we simply multiply the number of students enrolled in The Other School in 2010-2011 by the so-called gap of $10,700 claimed by The Other School, we get a figure of over $7 million—nearly double the annual fund goal of $4.2 million! If that surprises and perplexes you, as it should, then here's another little experiment that will really bring the point home: All of you private school parents reading this, please get out the latest fundraising brochure from your child's school. It will most certainly have a "gap" figure listed in the brochure as a central part of the school's "pitch." Now, simply multiply the overall enrollment in your child's school by the gap figure claimed by the school. The bottom line figure you arrive at in this simple calculation will be, I promise you, nowhere near the annual fund goal that your child's school claims it *needs* for the present school year—a sure indication that annual fund goals, on the one hand, and actual needs, on the other, have nothing in common! Private schools simply determine annual fund goals—and by doing so, the "gap"—by adding a convenient 5-6 percent to last year's goal. The annual fund goal, therefore—$4.2 million, for example, sought by The Other School—has no direct relationship whatsoever to the *actual needs* over at The Other School. Rather, it represents the amount The Other School can comfortably and reasonably raise based on prior experience. If prior experience indicated it could raise *twice* that amount, The Other School would surely do so—and happily spend it as well!

> **PRINCIPLE #4. Voluntary contributions to the operating budget of a private school (the typical annual fund) always lead to overspending—prompting in turn the need for more, and therefore *increased*, voluntary giving. As a result, voluntary contributions drive *up* the cost of tuition—never *lower* it, as universally claimed.**

This principle, written as it is in the form of cautionary advice, has everything to do with the "teleology" or "mindset" of schools that raise large amounts in annual giving and have large endowments in addition to large tuitions. Schools with these sorts of "wealthy" profiles invariably fall prey to the mentality that no amount of spending is too much—after all, the annual fund will bail them out. Running ever-larger deficits by these wealthy schools poses no real danger to their health and well-being (or so it might seem). The "teleology" of this situation reminds me of a wonderfully revealing story told by a reporter about a chance encounter with the legendary Texas billionaire H. L. Hunt. As this reporter tells the story, he chanced upon H. L. Hunt while changing planes in a Texas airport shortly after rumors started circulating in the Texas newspapers about H. L.'s youngest son's gambling losses in Las Vegas. The reporter asked H. L. what he thought about his son's losing over a $1 million gambling in Las Vegas during the past year. H. L. is reported to have replied: "By golly! I'm going to have to have a serious talk with that boy, cause at that rate he's liable to go broke in 250 years!" Losing a million dollars a year in Las Vegas to H. L.'s youngest son simply meant getting more money from daddy. Running an ever-larger deficit to a private school means no more than getting more from its wealthy parents—hence, the teleological cause of overspending in any private school that has the means—i.e., willing parents—to bail them out each year in the form of annual giving.

PRINCIPLE #5: Tuition income should always be for the present, and all voluntary giving only for the future.

This is the simplest, yet most important and most fundamental of all the 12 principles outlined here. If only this one principle were consistently followed by every private school (and college), then every school would be continually and consistently improving and growing over the years, as we have and continue to do. Tuition income should strictly and only be used for operations, and voluntary giving should strictly and only be used for capital growth and improvements. Unfortunately, ever-increasing amounts of voluntary giving are used by private schools to *operate* on a yearly basis, to close the so-called "gap" in the operating budget. This approach to "balancing" a school's budget is self-defeating and shortsighted at best and has reached alarming proportions, as we have seen, in the case of many private schools. If heads do not have the ability or willingness to rein in these ever-larger gaps, then trustees need to erect the necessary barriers before it is too late for many schools. In fact, I can't think of a simpler or more effective way for a board of trustees of a private school to carry out its fiduciary responsibilities than by erecting clear and unbridgeable barriers between operating expenditures on the one hand and capital on the other—or between tuition income on one side of the financial ledger and voluntary, tax-deductible gifts on the other.

PRINCIPLE #6: Endowments are to colleges and universities what annual funds are to private schools. Therefore, ever-expanding endowments and ever-increasing annual funds both create a false sense of security and well-being, while in reality the wealthier a school becomes, the more dependent—not less— it becomes on voluntary giving.

All that we have had to say about private K-12 schools and their reliance on annual funds applies equally to colleges and their reliance on endowment income to close their respective operating budgets. Surprisingly, as I point out in my chapter "The Endowment Trap," endowments are almost always underfunded, or soon become underfunded as the years go on. Hence, endowments, just as annual funds, ultimately drive up the costs of tuition and never lower these costs as universally advertised. This then is the answer in a nutshell to the puzzling question as to why the most heavily endowed schools in the world have the heftiest tuitions while at the same time the greatest need to raise ever larger amounts of money!

Both private schools and colleges find themselves equally caught on the horns of a dilemma, so to speak: Both need to raise increasing amounts of money each year just to break even, but by doing so, they end up creating the need for yet more money the following year, and so on and so forth. Private schools and colleges are caught in a vicious and self-defeating cycle of greater and greater need, with only marginal growth in the end for all their success in fundraising. In short, the conventional model of operating a school on ever-increasing amounts of voluntary giving is flawed at it roots and needs to be fundamentally re-examined before that sad, but inevitable day arrives when all growth in the form of capital expenditures—new buildings, investments in new programs, science centers and so on—comes to a grinding halt in the face of constantly accelerating operating expenses. If this all sounds overly alarming or exaggerated, I bring your attention to a little publicized but telling report recently released by *Bloomberg News*. This report should make national headlines, and certainly should be required reading for all college, university, and private schools that are overly dependent on endowments for their day-to-day survival. In brief, after the 2008 "crash," the 20 institutions surveyed, all among the most heavily endowed colleges and universities in America, led by Harvard, Yale and Princeton with Stanford and Cornell close behind, borrowed in the form of tax-exempt bonds the grand total of $7.5 billion—largely to continue operating their schools on a day-to-day basis, in effect, to maintain business as usual. Yes, according to Bloomberg, among 20 of the most heavily endowed colleges alone, this vast sum of money was borrowed, not to build towards a uniquely great future that could not otherwise be afforded, but largely to keep operating as usual. In the army they used to call this "Hurry up to stand still."

In sum, if this level of borrowing is required by our wealthiest colleges and universities every time the markets hit a rough patch simply to maintain the status quo, then these very same colleges and universities, irrespective of their lofty reputations for excellence and leadership, ought to re-examine, in my humble view, their respective financial models. It goes without saying that well-endowed private schools with ever-larger annual fund needs ought to do the same.

> **PRINCIPLE #7: At any private school where the endowment is as great or greater than the operating budget (all the best known schools), the amount of waste each school produces each year is equivalent—at a minimum—to its annual fund. This is the centerpiece of all these principles and is otherwise known as "Richard's Rule of Thumb."**

To determine if my favorite principle applies to your favorite school, say the one you attended or the one your child presently attends, you don't even have to leave your armchair. Just take out the school's latest annual giving report and make the following simple calculations: Check to see if the size of the endowment at your child's school is equal to or greater than its operating budget. If that is the case, then in all likelihood the amount of money your child's school is wasting on administrative bloat and duplication is going to be roughly equivalent to the amount your school is seeking to raise in annual giving.

Now, to actually *prove* that all this money is being wasted on non-academic and unnecessary positions, you have to do a bit more work. The simple way to *prove* or *disprove* the accuracy of "Richard's Rule of Thumb" as it applies to a particular school is to look at that school's operating budget. It would not take long to find or not find the "unnecessary" administrative positions scattered throughout the bureaucracy. In all probability, however, the head of the school in question is not going to let you have a peek at the school's operating budget, even on a short-term basis. Consequently, you will have to go through the somewhat convoluted and arduous process I followed with The Other School in order to identify all the waste and duplication that I predict is occurring at any school whose endowment is greater than its operating budget—true of most of the best-known private schools in New York City. (By the way, I'm happy to do the analysis for you, if your head of school would kindly send me a copy of the latest operating budget.)

> PRINCIPLE #8: Always make the "right gap," namely the gap between administrative and academic expenses, grow ever wider, while at the same time make the "wrong gap," namely between tuition income and operating expenses, grow ever smaller.

I call this principle the "Categorical Imperative of a Balanced Budget." You simply cannot manage a school in a financially successful manner without having your administrative expenses grow at a substantially lower rate than your academic expenses, which automatically creates the *right* gap and not the *wrong* gap. The right gap for any school—college, university, or private secondary school—is between academic expenses on the one hand and administrative on the other (see the graph on page 206). However, the direct opposite has been the defining characteristic of most schools of all kinds, including public, over the last three to four decades. Everywhere you look, you find that administrative costs have far outpaced academic, from salaries to space to number of employees. Just recently, *The Chronicle of Higher Education* published a national survey designed to calculate the average growth of these two areas, academic and administrative—the two most costly areas of any college or university—and the unsurprising discovery was that administrative costs have outpaced academic costs by an extraordinary margin of 50 percent over the last 30 years. In other words, an enormously greater proportion of the available funds at the college and university levels has gone towards greater and greater administrative expenses, from salaries to facilities and space—and not towards better faculty salaries and instructional programs. Is there any mystery therefore as to why the quality of our colleges and universities has not kept pace with the ever-rising costs of tuition and fees?

Now, while it is somewhat understandable that administrative bloat and duplication have found their way into the inner workings of large universities, it is nevertheless surprising to think that the same problems exist, albeit on a much smaller scale, in the cloistered world of private, K-12 education. Unfortunately, the answer is yes, and the sooner the situation is recognized and dealt with it, the sooner these schools can achieve true *financial sustainability*—and kick the *unsustainable* habit of relying on more and more voluntary giving to solve their problems.

PRINCIPLE #9: Hire the fewest number of administrators and pay them each as much as possible.

While it might seem disarmingly simplistic, Principle #9 is one of the best steps I have taken in my 31 years as headmaster and one of the best pieces of advice I can offer to others. Not only will it save enormous amounts of money for any school, it will create an administrative structure that is exponentially more streamlined, efficient, and happy as well. You would think that an administration kept at a bare-bones level would ultimately produce stress and exhaustion, and therefore unhappy staff. However, the opposite is true, as any parent or outside evaluator will confirm—not to mention our own employees. Speaking on behalf of the 19-member evaluating committee at the end of our last NYSAIS 10-year evaluation, the visiting committee chair asserted in her very first comments to our school community: "We were unanimous in feeling that this was the happiest school environment we have ever experienced!" And the committee went on to make clear that this included students, faculty, parents, and staff. As I have already pointed out, our business and development offices are a mere fraction of what you will find at other private schools in the city, even among those considerably smaller than Columbia Grammar.

In 1981 we had a budget of approximately $1 million. Today our budget is over $55 million annually, the largest private school budget among schools in Manhattan and the third-largest among the five boroughs. We have only one additional person in the business office and one in development, though our fundraising exceeded $7 million last year and $20 million over the last three years—it totaled less than $25,000 in 1981! And our headmaster's office is no larger—one head and one assistant/secretary—than it was 31 years ago, though the school has more than quadrupled in size. Indeed, the administrative structure throughout the school reflects our philosophy that "less is more."

Lastly, a streamlined administration has another virtue that in many ways defines our school environment: Keeping all management to a minimum encourages us to focus on our priority: the needs of students and faculty. Students and faculty alike have immediate access to those of us in a position to solve a problem or answer a question. There are no layers of bureaucracy between students, faculty, and parents on the one hand and a director or headmaster or chief financial officer on the other. There are very few meetings, even fewer memos, and even fewer committees. In brief, the fewest number of administrators paid as much as possible is one of the most important keys to a financially well-run and happy school. The stoic insight that "less is more" has never been truer than when it comes to a modern bureaucracy!

PRINCIPLE #10: Annual giving is in reality equivalent to long-term debt.

Annual giving and long-term debt are simply two sides of the same coin! Increasing the annual fund—something every private school routinely does each year—is equivalent to increasing a school's long-term debt, with the dubious distinction of having nothing to show for it the following year. It is understandably hard to appreciate this principle at first glance, especially when annual giving continually pours into your school's coffers, seemingly in endless amounts—and best of all, solves all your *immediate* problems. The Other School, for example, had little difficulty, I assume, in raising its annual fund goal of $4.2 million, found money, so to speak. Next year it will raise somewhere around $4.6 million, $5 million the year after, and so on *ad infinitum*—or not? The point here, however, is that The Other School *must* raise this money; in other words, it is far from "found money," but in fact money that The Other School is *dependent* upon! The annual fund at any private school—not just at The Other School—is equivalent to money owed, money that must be *repaid* year in and year out—not only a recurring debt, but an ever-increasing debt. Annual funds, regardless of how schools naïvely view them, are built into the core of a school's operating budget, a financial obligation no different from a loan owed to the local bank, or annual rent, or any other recurring debt.

This all reminds me of the story of the fellow who walks into a bank to ask for a loan. The officer of course asks him why he needs a loan, and the fellow replies, "I just want to borrow enough money to get out of debt!" The moral of this story for private school heads is simply that the Annual Fund, while it gets you out of debt for the present year, does no more good for the institution than the loan did for this poor soul who found himself in debt. Both the institution and the poor fellow who approached the bank for a loan will find themselves off course. In brief, the next time you sit down to write that "annual fund appeal letter," think of it as creating yet more long-term debt for your school. And Dear Private School Parent: Next fall when you once again receive your "annual fund appeal letter," think of it as *involuntary*—as opposed to *voluntary*, which the letter will misleadingly claim. You have no real choice: if you don't "close the gap" as the letter warns, your child won't get the education he or she deserves, which is certainly not my definition of "voluntary!"

PRINCIPLE #11: Waste in any bureaucracy always grows exponentially, never arithmetically.

One would assume, quite naturally, that waste would grow arithmetically. In other words, that as you *add* positions, you *add* waste—hence, the total amount of waste in any system is more or less an easy exercise in adding up the number of duplicative or unnecessary positions and calculating their costs. We carried out a similar exercise when we calculated the costs of unnecessary administrative positions—at least relative to Columbia Grammar and Prep's way of operating—over at The Other School. The fact is, however, that administrative bloat and duplication always costs a school (or indeed any bureaucracy) much *more* than the simple sum of the wasteful positions identified. While most waste can be identified and understood in this simple mathematical fashion, much also lives in a mysterious netherland of bureaucratic life—a fifth dimension so to speak. Waste breeds waste in uniquely bureaucratic ways that are largely hidden from view and difficult to ferret out, much less estimate their real costs.

For one thing, bureaucrats make work for other bureaucrats, administrators for other administrators in ways that are totally unique to the realm of bureaucracies. That much we know and has already been shown to us by C. Northcote Parkinson in his wonderful and humorous masterpiece, *Parkinson's Law*. What we don't know, however, is how to *calculate* what all this work created exclusively by and for and within a bureaucracy itself actually *costs*. I am referring here to the bureaucratic and administrative waste that is perniciously hidden from view and resides quietly in the recesses of every bureaucracy, in its DNA, if you will. One can recognize it immediately when we see it, but it seems almost impossible to figure out how to analyze its costs. We can't even figure out whether it's something minor or monumental when we run across it face to face. We run across countless examples of this subtle, but uniquely bureaucratic waste in our daily lives in the most ordinary circumstances, since, for better or for worse, life has become increasingly bureaucratic in all walks. For example, I recently lost my senior (half-fare) MetroCard and called the MTA, as instructed by its Web site, for a replacement. I spoke to a very nice lady who took all my information and politely assured me that a replacement card would be sent to me in 4-6 weeks (By the way, it actually took 11 weeks!) I politely thanked her and hung up, but was once again struck by the "hidden waste" in every bureaucracy. This incident reminded me of the heyday of AT&T's monopoly on phones and phone service—everything took 45 days to process! You were owed an adjustment on your phone bill—45 days to process! If you needed a change in service, once again—45 days to process, and so on! The larger and more entrenched a bureaucracy, the more you find the tell-tale signs of hidden waste and inefficiency. It's no wonder that the expression holds true: "If you have something that needs to be done, and done soon, give it to a busy person." Bureaucracies grow until everyone is no longer *busy*—and therefore, there is never anyone to whom you can give something to be done—if you want it to be done in a timely manner. In brief, the total amount of waste produced by any bureaucracy—and schools, even our cloistered little private schools, as well, are no exception—is always greater than the sum of its parts, even if you can't exactly calculate it. This fifth dimension of bureaucratic waste, this largely hidden realm where bureaucrats make work for each other, is the true source, I suggest, in modern terms, of the commonplace expression "hidden waste."

PRINCIPLE #12: Always Run Your School as a Business!

Yes, a school is a business, and no, "business" is not a bad word when applied to a private school. Our business is to offer the highest quality education possible for all our children in the most cost-effective ways possible: the best teachers paid as much as possible, the best and safest facilities maintained at the highest levels, and a diverse student body supported through ever-larger amounts of financial aid. All these essential ingredients that go into making and maintaining an excellent school are becoming ever-more costly, and therefore managing a school successfully over the long run, especially during times of financial strains and stresses, as we are facing in today's economy, requires a business perspective, not to mention expertise and experience, at the top—both among school heads and trustees alike. Running a school successfully in today's environment has everything to do with managing the school's finances as a business, and these key principles constitute, based on my own experience over the past three decades, the *sine qua non* of a successfully run school. Some of my principles can serve to operate a school (1, 2, 5, 8, and 9), while others are simply cautionary guidelines (3, 4, and 12), and yet others are simply good advice based on my experience over many years of running an expanding private school in a highly competitive environment. But no matter how they are characterized, taken together, these Twelve Principles constitute the conceptual framework for a fiscally well-managed school (or college or business or government). And each principle, in its own unique way, reflects the modus operandi of our school, and as a group answers the question as to why Columbia Grammar and Prep School, facing insolvency and under-enrollment in those dark days in the early 1980s, survived to become one of New York City's most successful private schools. And I am confident these Twelve Principles will help any school do the same.

HOW DO YOU DEFINE SUCCESS?

My admittedly audacious claim that these Twelve Principles constitute together the *sine qua non* of a fiscally well-managed school will likely strike most readers—and certainly other school heads—as a gross exaggeration, if not an outright falsehood. There are obviously many successful and fiscally responsible private schools within walking distance of Columbia Grammar, much less the five boroughs of New York City, not to mention all across America. So how can I possibly argue with any credibility that not a single private school can be successful without following my Twelve Principles, when indeed there are all these examples of successful schools throughout New York City violating each and every one of these principles on a daily basis?

I admit there seems to be a contradiction here, at least on the surface. None of these other schools follows any of these so-called "principles" much less all of them, and many of these schools are at the same time quite obviously successful—or at least appear to everyone to be so, from the most reputable accrediting agencies to the general public. So how are we going to make any practical sense of my seemingly contradictory position—that these schools, despite appearances to the contrary, are not actually "successful"—especially since my claim so obviously flies in the face of everyone else's judgment?

My answer in a word is that the definition of "success," which is so routinely applied to these schools, needs to be re-examined—and ultimately redefined. The simple fact is that the so-called "success" of these well-endowed private schools is totally and fundamentally dependent on the willingness of each of these schools to operate with ever larger deficits and on their ability to raise ever increasing sums of money each year through annual giving to balance their budgets. In the same vein, no one is foolish enough to claim that many of our largest and heretofore "successful" banks are nevertheless still "successful" when the only definition of success applicable to them is premised on a bailout through TARP—a handout from the taxpayers of America. Similarly, annual funds, the fancy jargon of private school brochures notwithstanding, are nothing other than *bailouts* to private schools at the expense of parents. *Tax-paying Americans are to TARP-bailed-out-banks as tuition-paying parents are to annual fund- financed schools.* Or, to put the matter in the simplest and most direct terms: If it were not for the seemingly endless and ever-larger sums of voluntary giving each of these schools raises—and indeed, must raise—each year in order to balance their budgets, you would see far fewer so-called *successful* private schools in New York City or anywhere else for that matter.

Basically, as long as parents and trustees continue to make up for the annual deficits of private schools, school heads have as little to worry about as H. L. Hunt's youngest son. The consequences, if any, are pushed so far down the road that worrying about cutting costs seems downright pedestrian or even unbecoming. And for all I know, perhaps the money will simply never stop flowing, regardless of economic circumstances. However, even if that's so, the bottom line is that bailing out private schools each year in the form of multi-million dollar infusions of voluntary, tax-deductible dollars is not my notion of a successful private school—and shouldn't be anyone else's for that matter. We all want to believe that our august and long-standing accrediting agencies—the National Association of Independent Schools, with over 2,000 members and the New York State Association of Independent Schools, with over 100 members—know what they are doing when they give their blessings to these schools, but frankly I question their judgment. The fact is that the present model of operating and managing a private school, no matter how long-standing and professionally endorsed, is nevertheless essentially flawed and needs to be re-examined—along with their definition of "success."

Unfortunately, the accrediting agencies, led by NAIS and NYSAIS, simply reinforce these poor practices each and every time they put their respective seals of approval next to a school's name. What are the poor, unsuspecting, tuition-paying parents to believe under such circumstances, where the most trusted educational accrediting agencies are happily giving schools *carte blanche* to operate on an ever-larger deficit basis each year without even a peep of concern? And, at the same time, what are the trustees able to say in the face of these detailed and highly respected reviews by accrediting agencies—carried out every 10 years at every private school with such elaborate posturing and fanfare, not to mention time and expense? And all of this effort misses the bottom line of financial health, namely, to stop operating on ever-larger deficits and begin operating within the more sane and practical constraints of tuition income.

Even if parents and trustees have doubts about operating a school in this way, what can they say in the face of such long-standing practices and the unqualified endorsement of such highly regarded agencies as the New York Association of Independent Schools? But contrary to all this conventional wisdom, the bottom line is that NYSAIS is no more correct in its assessment of how a so-called "successful" school should operate than Moody's, or Standard and Poor's, and indeed the Securities and Exchange Commission, our most "trusted" federal watchdog, were correct in their assessment of how a "successful" bank should operate—much less which banks were "successful." These banks, it turned out, were successful under certain "ideal" circumstances: namely that property prices among other assets were continually increasing in value, which should never have been anyone's long term notion of success in the first place!

Similarly, private schools are successful only if you are willing to view them under "ideal" circumstances as well: when annual funds continue to grow ever larger each year and endowments keep producing unrealistic yields on their principal. However, both are unrealistic expectations over the long run, as any experienced agency or person should have known. Home prices have already fallen. Annual funds and endowment funds will ultimately decline, as well. Yes, the private school world is a small and insulated one, but its behavior nevertheless reflects the larger world in which we live. Citicorp, AIG, and Lehman Brothers are simply larger and more complex versions of our private schools, living on deficits and borrowed money, as they do, even if in the case of private schools we give "borrowed money" the fancy name of annual giving. Voluntary giving is essentially a handout that serves no better purpose than to provide a timely and much-needed, though short term, cover for the basic flaws in a school's operating budget and leaves the school every bit as dependent the following year on an even larger annual fund (bailout) than the year before.

One of these days, and perhaps sooner than we might have expected, these ever-larger bailouts might well not be there to "balance" the budgets of all those schools routinely viewed as otherwise "successful." After all, parents can't be expected every year *ad infinitum* to foot the bills for private schools that irresponsibly run ever-larger deficits, especially when those deficits are unnecessary. At some point the goose (generous parents) might well stop laying those golden eggs (annual funds). It is wishful thinking to assume that the sub-prime mortgage fiasco is the only fiscal danger lurking in the wings. There are many circumstances that could well lead to a significant decline in the willingness or ability of parents to "voluntarily" give ever larger sums to private schools for no other reason than the necessity of balancing their budgets and proclaiming "success." When that day arrives, it is quite possible that private school parents—and hopefully our overly accommodating accrediting agencies, as well—will all be forced to re-think the present definition of a "successful private school." I am reminded here of Margret Thatcher's famous—and very appropriate—observation: "The basic problem with Socialism (annual funds) is that sooner or later you run out of other peoples' money!"

A CHART IS WORTH A THOUSAND WORDS

This then is my definition of a successful school: a school where every dollar given to it on a tax-deductible, voluntary basis, is used exclusively for capital improvements, never to operate the school—never, in other words, to substitute for tuition. To show you in a nutshell what can happen—and indeed will happen—at any school that lives by this definition over time, I offer you the following profile of CGPS over the past 31 years:

CAPITAL EXPENDITURES ON NEW BUILDING AND BROWNSTONE PURCHASES/RENOVATIONS		
	Date	Cost in Millions
High School Building (38,500 square feet)	1984–85	$6.5
20 West 94 Brownstone (6,000 square feet)	1986–87	$0.8
36 West 93 Building (45,000 square feet)	1995–96	$12.5
High School Extension (30,000 square feet)	2001–02	$16.5
36 West 94 Brownstone (5,500 square feet)	2004–05	$6.2
30 West 94 Brownstone (5,500 square feet)	2009–10	$7.2
32 West 94 Brownstone (5,500 square feet)	2010–11	$8.3
34 West 94 Brownstone (5,500 square feet)	2011–12	$8.0
Grammar School Expansion: New Gym, Walkway System, Outdoor Play Yard and Rooftop Science Center (6,000 square feet)	2011–12	$12.5
Original Building (18,500 square feet) Renovation	2012–13	$2.5
Total Costs for 10 Major Capital Projects		$81
In addition, we have carried out countless improvements, large and small, to our existing plant, from new libraries and cafeterias, to a fully refurbished swimming pool, computer labs, two computer centers and science and technology renovations.		$9.5
GRAND TOTAL		$90.5

Against this total of $90 million in actual dollars spent on capital improvements over three decades, we have raised, during this same period, slightly more than $90 million in voluntary giving, all of which has gone towards our ongoing effort to create the finest physical plant possible for our students. Most importantly, all of our capital expenditures have been paid for in full, with not a single dollar in outstanding debt today—proof positive that we have lived on tuition alone all these years and used 100 percent of our voluntary giving on capital improvements. And if you look at what we have accomplished in today's dollars, you can proudly and accurately say that we built a $250 million physical plant (in today's dollars) paid for in full, starting out back in 1981 in a state of insolvency with no real fundraising capacity at all. But this level of growth and renewal could not and would not have happened, even under the most favorable of circumstances, had we not learned to live—and live happily—on tuition alone and to use all of our voluntary donations for capital projects!

Operating our school successfully on tuition alone allowed us to use every generous dollar given to the school on a tax-deductible basis, over $90 million, for the purpose it was intended—not to fill a hole in the operating budget, the so-called "gap"—but to provide a better future for the school and the children we serve. Our 33 years of growth and renewal—our buildings, our lack of debt, our high teacher salaries and benefits, and our happy student body—can all stand in testament to the extraordinary magic of voluntary giving when it is directed exclusively and appropriately towards its original goal: a brighter future for our students and our school—and never misdirected towards "closing a gap." And I cannot provide a clearer or more direct proof that we have operated all these years on tuition alone than by the fact that $90 million was raised in voluntary giving and $90 million was spent on capital improvements. With no endowment to speak of, that leaves tuition as the *only* source of income for our operations over these three decades of offering the very finest college preparatory program possible.

And while all voluntary giving went toward capital growth and renewal, the ever-widening gap between academic expenses on the one hand and administrative expenses on the other allows us to direct an ever-larger proportion of our annual tuition increases towards improved faculty salaries. The net result of this circumstance is that we were able to increase faculty salaries on average eight percent a year for nine consecutive years, moving us to the forefront of faculty compensation in New York City.

In brief, we had no need whatsoever for annual funds to operate our school successfully and at the same time no need of endowment income to balance our budget. On the reverse side of the financial ledger, we had no need of tuition income to build our many new buildings or renovate our old and, in the end, no debt to burden our school's future. This, in a nutshell, is my definition of a *successful* school.

A NEW PARADIGM FOR PRIVATE SCHOOLS

The first and most important step a school can take to put itself on a strong financial footing, as I have tried to make clear throughout this book, is to eliminate deficit spending—a school's dependency on annual giving as part of its operating budget. Contrary to what schools might fear, namely, that the loss of annual giving income will by necessity drive *up* the cost of tuition, by eliminating annual giving—a school's unrestricted overdraft checking account—heads of school will be forced to learn how to operate within a more efficient administrative structure, thereby actually driving *down* the cost of tuition. The self-discipline required for this "new management philosophy" will carry over into other areas of school life as well and give the head of school the confidence needed to believe that a school's financial needs can and will be met first and foremost through "controlling costs" at the *beginning* of the school year—and not as they are presently met, through increased fundraising and endowment income at the *end*. And the bottom-line benefit of this new approach to running a school is that it will free up fundraising for capital projects and a stronger future.

There is, thankfully, a simple and straightforward way of conceptualizing this new approach to managing a school. The wrong way, to begin with, is to think in terms of a "gap" between operating costs and tuition income. If a school persists in thinking in these terms, it will not only continue to run deficits, but will concentrate the bulk of its energy on closing that deficit—or "gap"—through fundraising, ultimately a losing proposition. The "right gap," however, is the one between *administrative costs* on the one hand and *academic costs* on the other. Rather than *closing* the so-called gap between tuition and the cost of educating a student—*a gap that should not exist in the first place*—a school should focus rather on *widening* the gap between administrative and academic costs. If this gap is steadily widened year after year, a school will automatically close the gap between tuition and the so-called real cost of educating a student— *and the annual fund will disappear forever*. It will become a soon-to-be forgotten relic of the past and of past practices. It is truly as simple as reducing your administrative overhead in direct proportion to your present annual fund and presto, no more deficit! And an added benefit of no small consequence is that the board of trustees, when it wants to understand at a glance whether a school is growing successfully or not—headed in the right direction or not—need only look at a simple chart like this one:

PERCENTAGE INCREASES

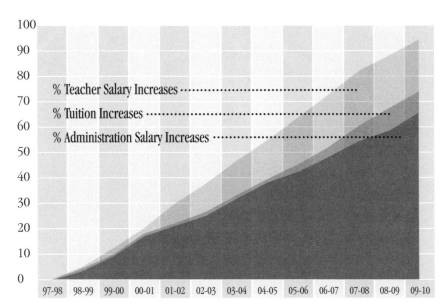

This chart shows how we at Columbia Grammar and Prep gradually increased the "right gap" between our academic and administrative salaries over the past dozen years. I would venture that any private school in New York constructing the same chart based on its own annual budget will discover, without doubt and perhaps much to its surprise, that the administrative line has gone up much higher than the academic over the years. This will show (and indeed should convince) that school that it is headed in the *wrong* direction. It will also illustrate where their annual giving dollars are actually being spent.

With a straightforward and foolproof graph like this, a school head, trustee, or even the most uninvolved and casual parent can get an honest and timely picture of where the school has been and where it is headed in basic financial terms. You needn't be an MBA with a sophisticated math background and certainly not a rocket scientist to stay on top of the financial basics of a well-managed and successful—and totally sustainable—school. All you have to do as a school head or trustee is to make sure that the lines representing academic costs and administrative costs are getting wider apart each year than closer together. Of course, if you find out the bad news that they are actually getting closer together, then you have your work cut out for you—and that's to reduce administrative costs accordingly. It's a difficult process, but at least you know what you have to do to put your school on a truly sustainable path.

Pie charts by the way give you little useful information, even if they are accurate. At best, a pie chart is a static picture of a school's finances in the most simplistic terms at a given moment: 60 percent spent in the academic areas, 20 percent administrative, 10 percent maintenance, etc.—covering a single year. The interesting question is not what was spent the past year on academics, for example, but whether it was more or less than what was spent during the previous year and whether there is a trend upwards or downwards. It is the trend that counts, and if schools were forthright enough to publish for parents, faculty and trustees alike, the actual trends that represent the school's last 10 years, let's say, or better yet 15 or 20, then interesting and helpful questions could be raised. The graph that I recommend above, unlike pie charts, unambiguously tells you whether or not more money is being spent (and what proportion) on each student versus what is being spent on administration—*as a trend*. Once you rid yourself of the infamous pie chart and plot out your trends based on ten years or more of audit reports, you will finally know unequivocally whether you are headed in the right direction or not.

Your task, then, as a "reformed" school head, will be to reverse the directions of these two distinct worlds, administrative and academic respectively. In other words, you need to begin cutting back in administrative costs, mainly salaries, so that the administrative line on your graph barely rises from year to year. At the same time, you need to put all savings and all voluntary giving into the academic areas and capital projects, from greatly increased salaries to better facilities. When you look at your chart five and certainly ten years down the road, you will see that as the "right gap" gets wider, the "wrong gap" between tuition and the so-called "real costs" of educating a student becomes narrower, until it finally disappears for good—and good riddance!

The chart will also simplify and improve communication and dialogue between trustees and school heads immeasurably. The board will never need to involve itself, as appropriately it should not, in the details of the school's operation, or to meddle in the head's independence in running the school. Once a year, perhaps twice at most, usually after the annual audit, the board simply needs to look at this single chart. If these two lines—administrative on the one hand and academic on the other—are not getting wider apart, then further questions and perhaps intervention would be called for by the board. However, as long as these two lines are widening, the board can rest assured that in general terms the school is operating successfully, with its resources directed toward providing a better education for its students and towards a financially stronger and more efficient school for the future. And over a period of time, five to ten years, though perhaps longer, the telltale "gap" will disappear, much to every parent's delight and financial relief.

THREE DECADES: A SUMMARY		
	1981–1982	2012–2013
Enrollment	479	1,291
Operating Budget	$1,100,000	$52,500,000
Faculty and Staff	75	315
Student-Teacher Ratio	9.2:1	5.9:1
Starting Teacher Salaries	Bottom Tier of NYC Private Schools	#1 starting salary in NYC $72,000 with a master's, first-year teacher
Financial Aid	$93,000	$6.1 million
Total Giving	$70,000	$7 million
Major Capital Projects	None	**1985**: $6.5 million High School **1987**: $1.0 brownstone renovation **1995**: $13 million Middle School **2002**: $16.5 million high school addition **2005**: $5.4 million brownstone acquisition & renovation **2008**: $6.1 million new brownstone **2009**: $7.2 million new brownstone **2011**: $12.5 million construction of elevator/rooftop science center/ fourth gym/outdoor play area/ connection walkway system **2011**: $8 million brownstone **2012**: $2.5 million renovation of original building
Financial Profile	$700K in debt and technically insolvent	$250 million physical plant and NO DEBT!

THE CONCLUSION

"Habit, if not resisted, soon becomes necessity."–St. Augustine

We have now come to the close of our journey into private school finances and management. If this discussion has served any worthwhile purpose, I hope it has everything to do with how private schools spend–or misspend–the growing millions of tax-deductible dollars solicited each year largely from well-intentioned parents and alumni. The greatest generosity and goodwill imaginable exists in our private school communities. Indeed, no other country in the world can come close to our levels of voluntary support for schools and education in general–public, private, and parochial alike. However, all this generosity notwithstanding, too large a portion of this voluntary giving is serving in many schools no better purpose than to sustain their operating budgets with too little going towards growth and a better future–and therefore a better education for their students.

The time for change is long overdue. The days of closing the wrong gap–the gap between tuition on the one hand and the so-called "real" costs of education on the other–should come to an end. Put differently, private schools should quit soliciting their generous parents and alumni for the wrong-headed and unsustainable purpose of substituting voluntary donations for tuition income. Annual funds and similar fundraising programs should become a thing of the past and should stop serving as blank checks for poorly managed schools. Broadly speaking, schools need to begin weaning themselves from the overuse of deficit spending to solve all their financial problems.

At the same time, the days of widening the right gap–the gap between our all-important academic expenses on the one hand and the far less-important administrative expenses on the other–should begin in earnest. Unlike pie charts, the graph I suggest on page 206 will never mislead you: More and more financial support for the academic areas and less and less for the administrative will invariably illustrate that the two largest and most essential expenses in any school's budget are diverging ever farther apart, resulting in an ever-richer and more rewarding learning environment for students and an ever more streamlined and practical administration for faculty and parents—in short, a more successful and sustainable school.

This, in essence, is the message of this little book, and in the final analysis, the answer to the question so often asked of Columbia Grammar and Preparatory School: How did we go from insolvency and deep debt three decades ago to becoming one of the premier schools in New York City with a physical plant the envy of all with no debt whatsoever? While the story of our school's success is of course gratifying, the best message of all is that a similar future is well within the means of any private school, large or small, rich or poor. Every school, regardless of its circumstances, can greatly improve its prospects and begin building towards a much better future for its own students and faculty, starting today. Working within the broad parameters of our Twelve Principles, a school can be assured of spending all of its dollars—tuition and voluntary gifts alike—wisely with a view to a more successful and sustainable future. But if following the Twelve Principles seems too daunting or burdensome as a first step, then simply keep in mind the singular message that resonates throughout our own three decades of growth and renewal: Good things happen when you Mind the Gap!

FURTHER ACKNOWLEDGEMENTS

I don't know if it is common among authors, but I started this book a couple of years ago on the naïve assumption that it would take a few weeks—months at most—to write and would present few practical problems, not to mention conceptual ones. I am today a much chastened writer, with an abiding respect for the challenges—and surprises—any book, even one based as this is on years of personal experience, has in store for the unsuspecting writer. Perhaps the most important lesson learned is that you can't complete the task, or certainly can't do it as well as you would like, without the help of many talented and generous souls.

First of all, I want to acknowledge the invaluable and expert work of my editor, Alida Clemans, who not only organized the project in all its many details, but encouraged me throughout. Alida, simply put, was my "project-manager supreme," without whom the first draft would still be wasting away in my desk drawer! And she carried out the final and most painstaking aspect of finishing any book—the so-called (and endless) "final editing!" I am eternally grateful to Alida for sparing me that awful, but essential, chore.

Secondly, this book would never have become a reality without the invaluable efforts of Elaine Kingman, my assistant. Elaine not only carried out all of her other considerable duties during these past two years, but miraculously kept all my thoughts, changes, re-organizations, and brainstorms organized somehow in a coherent fashion, ultimately becoming the book you just finished reading. And she did all this without ever losing her patience or uttering a single complaint!

I owe Patrick Huyghe an immense thank you for editing the original collection of chapters, notes, and seemingly random thoughts into something that could honestly be called a book. Without his insights and highly skilled judgments, I would still be pondering the overall structure of this work. Patrick even suggested the title, which I first found unappealing but have now grown to love!

Frank Palazzolo did an absolutely superb job with the overall design and graphics. Frank is one of the most professional and talented designers I have ever worked with on any project. Simply put, he has a magical touch and an eye for capturing the spirit and essence of the task at hand.

And lastly, my warmest appreciation to five of my most talented and generous colleagues, who spent hours each proofreading the manuscript and offering invaluable suggestions throughout: John Bailin, Glenn Cramer, Janet Kraus, Monica Markovits, and Marvin Terban.

Photo: Blanca Millan

214

ABOUT THE AUTHOR

Dr. Richard J. Soghoian completed his undergraduate studies in philosophy at the University of Virginia and received a Ph.D. in philosophy from Columbia University in 1970. He taught philosophy at the University of Denver and served as Director of the Graduate School at Pratt Institute. Prior to becoming Headmaster of Columbia Grammar and Preparatory School in 1981, Dr. Soghoian served as Dean of the College and Vice President for Academic Affairs at Manhattanville College in Purchase, New York. He is the father of five children.

MIND THE GAP!

Editor: Alida Durham Clemans

Graphic Design: Frank Palazzolo, Design for Business

Printed by: Puritan Capital, Hollis, New Hampshire